孫子兵法

Position Perspective Opportunities Probability Situations Mistakes Momentum Rewards Vulnerabilities

VI

Sun Tzu's
Art of War
Playbook
Volume 6 of 9:
Situations

Gary
Gagliardi

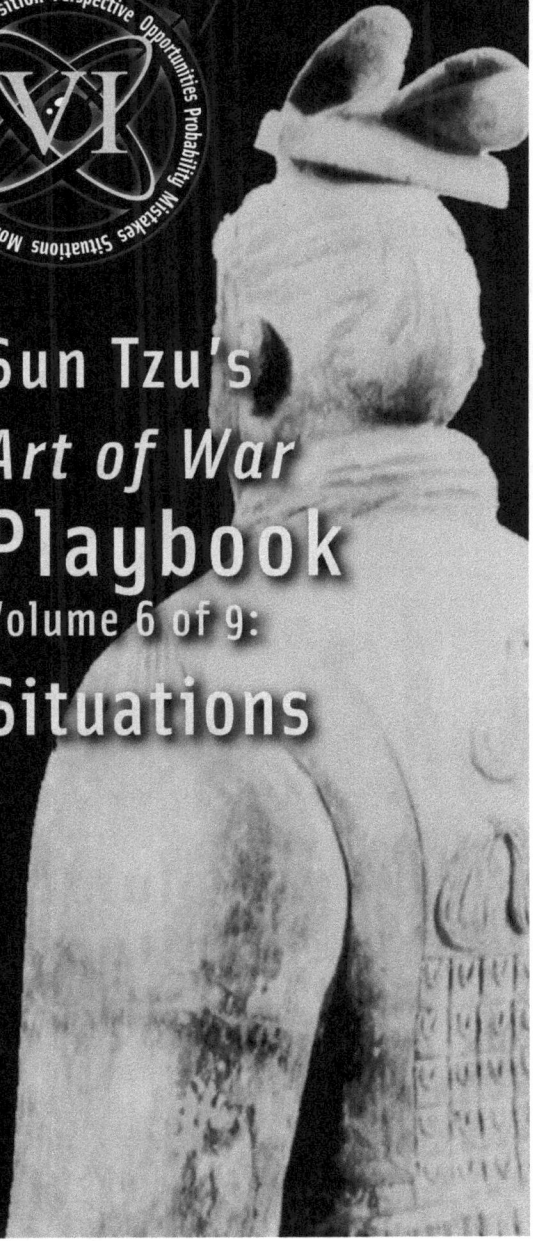

孫子

Sun Tzu's Art of War

兵法

Playbook

Volume Six: Situations

by Gary Gagliardi
The Science of Strategy Institute
Clearbridge Publishing

Published by
Science of Strategy Institute, Clearbridge Publishing
    suntzus.com   scienceofstrategy.org

First Print Edition
Library of Congress Control Number: 2014909969
Also sold as an ebook under the title Sun Tzu's Warrior Playbook
Copyright 2010, 2011, 2012, 2013, 2014 Gary Gagliardi
ISBN 978-1-929194-81-0(13-digit) 1-929194-81-1 (10-digit)

Originally published as a series of articles on the Science of Strategy Website, scienceofstratregy.org. and
later as an ebook on various sites.

PO Box 33772, Seattle, WA 98133
Phone: (206)542-8947 Fax: (206)546-9756
beckyw@clearbridge.com
garyg@scienceofstrategy.org

Manufactured in the United States of America.
Interior and cover graphic design by Dana and Jeff Wincapaw.
Original Chinese calligraphy by Tsai Yung, Green Dragon Arts, www.greendragonarts.com.

Publisher's Cataloging-in-Publication Data
Sun-tzu, 6th cent. B.C.
Strategy, positioning, success, probability
    [Sun-tzu ping fa, English]
    Art of War Playbook / Sun Tzu and Gary Gagliardi.
    p.197 cm. 23
    Includes introduction to basic competitive philosophy of Sun Tzu

Clearbridge Publishing's books may be purchased for business, for any promotional use,
or for special sales.

Contents

Playbook Overview

Note: This overview is provided for those who have not read the previous volume of Sun Tzu's Art of War Playbook. *It provides an brief overview of the work in general and the general concepts framing the first volume.*

Sun Tzu's **The Art of War** is less a "book" in the modern Western sense than it is an outline for a course of study. Like Euclid's Geometry, simply reading the work teaches us very little. Sun Tzu wrote in in a tradition that expected each line and stanza to be studied in the context of previous statements to build up the foundation for understanding later statements.

To make this work easier for today's readers to understand, we developed the **Strategy Playbook**, the Science of Strategy Institute (SOSI) guidebook to explaining Sun Tzu's strategy in the more familiar format of a series of explanations with examples. These lessons are framed in the context of modern competition rather than ancient military warfare.

This Playbook is the culmination of over a decade of work breaking down Sun Tzu's principles into a series of step-by-step practical articles by the Institute's multiple award-winning author and founder, Gary Gagliardi. The original **Art of War** was written for military generals who understood the philosophical concepts of ancient China, which in itself is a practical hurdle that most modern readers cannot clear. Our **Art of War Playbook** is written for today's reader. It puts Sun Tzu's ideas into everyday, practical language.

The Playbook defines a new science of strategic competition aimed at today's challenges. This science of competition is designed as the complementary opposite of the management science that is taught in most business schools. This science starts, as Sun Tzu did himself, by defining a better, more complete vocabulary for discussing competitive situations. It connects the timeless ideas of Sun Tzu to today's latest thinking in business, mathematics, and psychology.

The entire Playbook consists of two hundred and thirty articles describing over two-thousand interconnected key methods. These articles are organized into nine different areas of strategic skill from understanding positioning to defending vulnerabilities. All together this makes up over a thousand pages of material.

Playbook Access

The Playbook's most up-to-date version is available as separate articles on our website. Live links make it easy to access the connections between various articles and concepts. If you become a SOSI Member, you can access any Playbook article at any time and access their links.

However, at the request of our customers, we also offer these articles as a series of nine eBooks. Each of the nine sections of the entire Playbook makes up a separate eBook, Playbook Parts One Through Nine. These parts flow logically through the Progress Cycle of listen-aim-move-claim (see illustration). Because of the dynamic nature of the on-line version, these eBooks are not going to be as current as the on-line version. You can see a outline of current Playbook articles here and, generally, the eBook version will contain most of the same material in the same order.

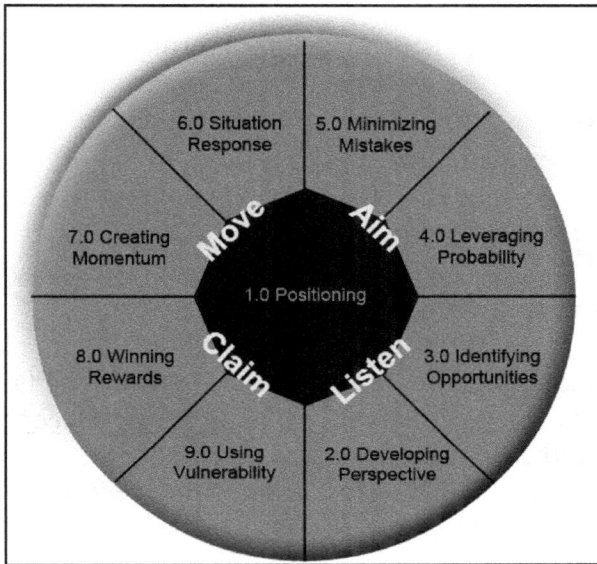

Nine categories of strategic skills define cycle that advances our positions:

1. Comparing Positions,

2. Developing Perspective,

3. Identifying Opportunities,

4. Leveraging Probability,

5. Minimizing Mistakes,

6. Responding To Situations,

7. Creating Momentum,

8. Winning Rewards, And

9. Defending Vulnerabilities.

Playbook Structure and Design

These articles are written in standard format including 1) the general principle, 2) the situation, 3) the opportunity, 4) the list of specific Art of War key methods breaking down the general principle into a series of actions, and 5) an illustration of the application of each of those key methods to a specific competitive situation. Key methods are written generically to apply to every competitive arena (business, personal life, career, sports, relationships, etc.) with each specific illustrations drawn from one of these areas.

A number identifies where each article appears in Playbook Structure. For example, the article <u>2.1.3 Strategic Deception</u> is the third article in the first section of the second book in the nine volumes of the Strategy Playbook. In our on-line version, these links are live, clicking on them brings you to the article itself. We provide them because the interconnection of concepts is important in learning Sun Tzu's system.

Playbook Training

Training in Sun Tzu's warrior skills does not entail memorizing all these principles. Instead, these concepts are used to develop exercises and tools that allow trainees to put this ideas in practice. While each rule is useful, the heart of Sun Tzu system is the methods that connect all the principles together. Training in these principles is designed to develop a gut instinct for how Sun Tzu's strategy is used in different situations to produce success. Principles are interlinked because they describe a comprehensive conceptual mental model. Warrior Class training puts trainees in a situation where they must constantly make decisions, rewarding them for making decisions consist with winning productively instead of destructively.

About Positions

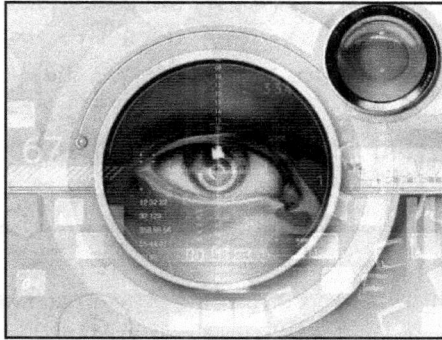

This first volume of Sun Tzu's Playbook focuses on teaching us the nature of strategic positions. "Position awareness" gives you a framework for understanding your strategic situation relative to the conditions around you. It enables you to see your position as part of a larger environment constructed of other positions and the raw elements that create positions. Master Sun Tzu's system of comparing positions, you can understand which aspect of your position are secure and which are the most dynamic and likely to change.

Traditional strategy defines a "position" as a comparison of situations. Game theory defines is as the current decision point that is arrive at as the sum or result of all previous decisions, both yours and those of others. Sun Tzu's methods of positioning awareness are different. They force you to see yourself in the eyes of others. Using these techniques, you broaden your perspective by gathering a range of viewpoints. In a limited sense, the scope of your position defines your area of control within your larger environment. In traditional strategy, five elements--mission, climate, ground, command, and methods--define the dimensions in which competitors can be compared.

Competition as Comparison

Sun Tzu saw that success is based on comparisons. This comparison must take place whenever a choice is made. For Sun Tzu, competition means a comparison of alternative choices or "positions". Battles are won by positioning before they are fought. These positions provide choices for everyone involved. Good positions discourage others from attacking you and invite them to support you. Sun Tzu's system teaches us how to systematically build up our positions to win success in the easiest way possible.

Competing positions are compared on the basis many elements, both objective and subjective. Sun Tzu's strategy is to identify these points of comparison and to understand how to leverage them. Learning Sun Tzu's strategy requires learning the details of how positions are compared and advanced. Sun Tzu taught that fighting to "sort things out" is a foolish way to find learn the strengths and weaknesses of a position. Conflict to tear down opposing positions is the most costly way to win competitive comparisons.

Today's More Competitive World

In the complex, chaotic world of today, we can easily get trapped into destructive rather than productive situations. Even our smallest decisions can have huge impact on our future. The problem is that we are trained for yesterday's world of workers, not today's world of warriors. We are trained in the linear thinking of planning in predictable, hierarchical world. This thinking applies less and less to today's networked, more competitive world.

Following a plan is the worker's skill of working in pre-defined functions in an internal, stable, controlled environment. The competitive strategy of Sun Tzu is the warrior's skill of making good decisions about conditions in complex, fast-changing, competitive environments. Sun Tzu's strategic system teaches us to adapt to the unexpected events that are becoming more and more common in our lives. We live in a world where fewer and fewer key events are planned. Navigating our new world of external challenges requires a different set of skills.

Most of us make our decisions without any understanding of competition. The result is that most of us lose as many battles as we win, never making consistent progress. Events buffet us, turning us in one direction and then the other. Too often, we end up repeating our past patterns of mistakes.

The Science of Strategy Institute teaches you the warrior's skills of adaptive response. There are many organizations that teach planning and organization. The Institute is one of the few places in the world you can get learn competitive thinking, and the only place in the world, with a comprehensive Playbook.

Seeing Situations Differently

Sun Tzu taught that a warrior's decision-making was a matter of reflex. As we develop our strategic decision-making skills, the critical conditions in situations simply "pop" out at us. This isn't magic. The latest research on how decisions are made tells us a lot about why Sun Tzu's principles work. It comes from using patterns to retrain our mind to see conditions differently. The study of successful response arose from military confrontations, where every battle clearly demonstrated how hard it is to predict events in the real world. Sun Tzu saw that winners were always those who knew how to respond appropriately to the dynamic nature of their situation.

Sun Tzu's principles provides a complete model for the key knowledge for understanding conditions in complex dynamic environments. This model "files" each piece of data into the appropriate place in the big picture. As the picture of your situation fills in, you can identify the opportunities hidden within your situation.

Making Decisions about Conditions

Instead of focusing on a series of planned steps, Sun Tzu's principles are about making decisions regarding conditions. It concerns itself with: 1) identifying the relative strengths and weaknesses of competitive positions, 2) advancing positions leveraging opportunities, and 3) the types of responses to specific challenges that work the most frequently. Using Sun Tzu's principles, we call these three areas position awareness , opportunity development , and situation response . Each area that we master broadens your capabilities.

- Position awareness trains us to recognize that competitive situations are defined by the relationship among alternative positions. Developing this perspective never ends. It deepens throughout our lives.
- Opportunity development explores the ground, testing our perceptions. Only testing the edges of perspective through action can we know what is true.
- S ituation response trains us to recognize the key characteristics of the immediate situation and to respond appropriately. Only by practice, can we learn to trust the viewpoint we have developed.

Success in competitive environments comes from making better decisions every day. Sharp strategic reflexes flow from a clear understanding of where and when you use which competitive tools methods.

The Key Viewpoints

As an individual, you have a unique and valuable viewpoint, but every viewpoint is inherently limited by its own position. The result is that people cannot get a useful perspective on their own situations and surrounding opportunities. The first formula of positioning awareness involve learning what information is relevant. The most advanced techniques teach how to gather that information and put it into a bigger picture.

Most people see their current situations as the sum of their past successes and failures. Too often people dwell on their mistakes while simultaneously sitting on their laurels. Sun Tzu's strategy forces you to see your position differently. How you arrived at your current position doesn't matter. Your position is what it is. It is shaped by history but history is not destiny.

In this framework, the only thing that matters is where you are going and how you are going to get there. As you begin to develop your strategic reflexes, you start to think more and more about how to secure your current position and advance it.

Seeing the Big Picture

Most people see all the details of their lives, but they cannot see what those detail mean in terms of the big picture. As you master position awareness, you don't see your life as a point but as a path. You see your position in terms of what is changing and what resources are available. You are more aware of your ability to make decisions and your skills in working with others.

Most importantly, this strategic system forces you to get in touch with your core set of goals and values.

Untrained people usually see their life in terms of absolutes: successes and failures, good luck and bad, weakness and strength. As you begin to master position awareness, you begin to see all comparisons of strength and weakness are temporary and relative. A position is not strong or weak in itself. Its strength or weakness depends on how it compares or "fits" with surrounding positions. Weakness and strength are not what a position is, but how you use it.

The Power of Perspective

Positional awareness gives you the specialized vocabulary you need to understanding how situations develop. Mastering this vocabulary, you begin to see the leverage points connecting past and future. You replace vague conceptions of "strength," "momentum," and "innovation" with much more pragmatic definitions that you can actually use on a day to day basis.

Mastering position awareness also changes your relationships with other people. It teaches you a different way of judging truth and character. This methods allow you to spot self-deception and dishonest in others. It also allows you to understand how you can best work with others to compensate for your different weaknesses.

Once you develop a good perspective of position, it naturally leads you to want to learn more about how you can improve you position through the various aspects of opportunity development covered in the subsequent parts of the Strategy Playbook.

Seeing the Invisible

The "Nazca lines" are giant drawings etched across thirty miles of desert on Peru's southern coast. The patterns are only visible at a distance of hundreds of feet in the air. Below that, they look like strange paths or roads to nowhere. Just as we cannot see these lines without the proper perspective, people who master Sun Tzu's methods can <u>suddenly recognize situations</u> that were invisible to them before. Unless we have the right perspective, we cannot compare situations and positions successfully. The most recent scientific research explains why people cannot see these patterns for comparison without developing the network framework of adaptive thinking.[1]

Seeing Patterns

We can imagine patterns in chaotic situations, but seeing real pattern is the difference between success and failure. In our seminars, we demonstrate the power of seeing patterns in a number of exercises.

The <u>mental models</u> used by warrior give them "situation awareness." This situation awareness isn't just vague theory. Recent research shows that it can be measured in a variety of ways.[2] We now know that untrained people fall victim to a flow of confusing information because they don't know where its pieces fit. Those trained in Sun Tzu's mental models plug this stream of information quickly and easily into a bigger picture, transforming the skeleton's provided by Sun Tzu's system into a functioning awareness of your strategic position and its relation to other positions. Each piece of information has a place in that picture. As the information comes in, it fills in the picture, like pieces of a puzzle.

The ability to see the patterns in this bigger picture allows experts in strategy to see what is invisible to most people in a number of ways. They include:

- People trained in Art of War principles--<u>recognition-primed decision-making</u> --see patterns that others do not.
- Trained people can spot anomalies, things that should happen in the network of interactions but don't.
- Trained people are in touch with changes in the environment within appropriate time horizons.
- Trained people recognize complete patterns of interconnected elements under extreme time pressure.

Procedures Make Seeing Difficult

One of the most surprising discoveries from this research is that those who know procedures, that is, a linear view of events, alone have a ___more___ difficult time recognizing patterns than novices. An interesting study[3] examined the different recognition skills of three groups of people 1) experts, 2) novices, and 3) trainers who taught the standard procedures. The three groups were asked to pick out an expert from a group novices in a series of videos showing them performing a decision-making task, in this case, CPR. Experts were able to recognize the expert 90% of the time. Novices recognized the expert 50% of the time. The shocking fact was that trainers performed much worse that the novices, recognizing the expert only 30% of the time.

Why do those who know procedures fail to see what the experts usually see and even novices often see? Because, as research into <u>mental simulations</u> has shown, those with only a procedural model fit everything into that model and ignore elements that don't fit. In the above experiment, interviews with the trainers indicated that they assumed that the experts would always follow the procedural model. In real life, experts adapt to situations where unique conditions often trump procedure. Adapting to the situation rather than following set procedures is a central focus the form of strategy that the Institute teaches.

Missing Expected Elements

People trained to recognize the bigger picture beyond procedures also recognize when expected elements are missing from the picture. These anomalies or, what the cognition experts[4] describe as "negative cues" are invisible to novices *and* to those trained only in procedure. Without sense of the bigger pattern, people are focused too narrowly on the problem at hand. The "dog that didn't bark" from the Sherlock Holmes story, "Silver Blaze," is the most famous example of a negative cue. Only those working from a larger nonprocedural framework can expect certain things to happen and notice when they don't.

The ability to see what is missing also comes from the expectations generated by the mental model. Process-oriented models have the expectation of one step following another, but situation-recognition models create their expectations from signals in the environment. Research[5] into the time horizons of decision-makers shows that different time scales are at work. People at the highest level of organizations must look a year or two down the road, using strategic models that work in that timeframe, doing strategic planning. Decision-makers on the front-lines, however, have to react within minutes or even seconds to changes in their situation, working from their strategic reflexes. The biggest danger is that people get so wrapped up in a process that they lose contact with their environment.

Decisions Under Pressure

Extreme time pressure is what distinguishes front-line decision-making from strategic planners. One of the biggest discoveries in cognitive research[6] is that trained people do much better in seeing their situation instantly and making the correct decisions under time pressure. Researchers found virtually no difference between the decisions that experts made under time pressure when comparing them to decisions made without time pressure. That research also finds that those with less experience and training made dramatically worse decisions when they were put under time pressure.

The central argument for training our strategic reflexes is that our situation results, not from chance or luck, but from <u>the instant decisions</u> that that we all make every day. Our position is the sum of these decisions. If we cannot make the right decisions on the spot, when they are needed, our plans usually come to nothing. This is why we describe training people's strategic reflexes as helping them "do at first what most people only do at last."

The success people experience seeing what is invisible to others is dramatic. To learn more about how the strategic reflexes we teach differ from what can be planned, read about <u>the contrast between planning and reflexes here</u> . As <u>our many members report</u>, the success Sun Tzu's system makes possible is remarkable.

1 Chi, Glaser, & Farr, 1988, The Nature of Expertise, Erlbaum
2 Endsley & Garland, Analysis and Measurement of Situation Awareness
3 Klein & Klein, 1981, "Perceptual/Cognitive Analysis of proficient CPR Performance", Midwestern Psychological Association Meeting, Chicago.
4 Dr. David Noble, Evidence Based Research, Inc.In Gary Klein, Sources of Power, 1999
5 Jacobs & Jaques, 1991, "Executive Leadership".In Gal & Mangelsdofs (eds.), Handbook of Military Psychology, Wiley
6 Calder, Klein, Crandall,1988, "Time Pressure, Skill, and Move Quality in Chess". American Journal of Psychology, 101:481-493

About Responding to Situations

Competitive environments are uncertain. Competitors will always do something unexpected. Successful strategies must constantly adjust to these unpredictable conditions. Fortunately, the science of strategy lays out the most common ways situations change and how you should adjust your responses to them. This is the focus of this volume of Sun Tzu's Playbook.

We cannot completely understand any competitive situation. This is the information problem at the heart of all competition. The goal therefore is simply to understand the changing situation better than your competitors do. You can then use the dynamics of situations to control your opponents' behavior. This requires understanding the principles for identifying and reacting appropriately to changing conditions.

The Power of Choice

When you explore an opportunity, you cannot know what exact conditions you will encounter. Not only that, but those conditions will change as your venture continues toward its goal. Progress itself forces changes in the situation. A competitive campaign is like driving. You know where you want to go, but you have to deal with a wide variety of traffic conditions on the way. You constantly adjust the way you drive to accommodate the traffic you encounter.

You cannot succeed in pursuing any opportunity unless you can surmount the challenges you meet along the way. Consistent progress requires different types of adjustments. Every situation offers challenges, but you can always find a good response if you understand the deeper nature of those challenges and the general approach it requires. This knowledge allows you to react quickly to changing conditions.

Competitive situations may not follow a plan, but they do follow a pattern. The principles in this volume teach us that pattern. In each evolving situation, a different response is required. These key methods teach you those responses. Sometimes the right response is speed. Sometimes it is cooperation. Sometimes it is an act of desperation. You use the key methods in this volume to correctly diagnose the situation. This enables you to know generally how to respond. Adapting to situations in the appropriate way is the key to success.

The Nine Common Stages

This volume introduces you to nine predictable situations or stages that arise naturally in a competitive campaign. These situations can be described as early, middle, or late stages. Early on, you run into dissipating, easy, and contentious situations. Later on, you run into open, shared, and serious situations. Toward the end of a campaign, conditions become more challenging leading to difficult, limited, and, finally, desperate situations.

This volume, the principles for identifying each of this nine situations are explained in detail, but let us define these stages generally here to provide you some perspective:

- Before a campaign starts, you have to defend against outside threats and criticism. This is the dissipating stage.
- When you begin a new campaign, the idea can seem novel and exciting. This is the easy stage.
- When you start to see some success, competitors and rivals can want to take it from you. This is the contentious stage.
- When you can make progress while competitors are also finding their way, this is the open stage.
- Over time, you can discover that good partnerships are needed to support your position. This is the shared stage.

- As the project makes progress but without paying, critics can start sniping at your back. This is the serious stage.
- As time passes, you can run into unforeseeable barriers to making progress. This is the difficult stage.
- When a campaign is close to success, you can come to a key transition point. This is the limited stage.
- In the end, your success may require you to quickly commit all your resources. This is the final desperate stage.

There is nothing new in any of these situations. They have occurred a million times in competition, but every situation will not occur in every campaign. You cannot predict if or when they will occur.

Every change is a new opportunity to make the right decision. If you run into a problem at the beginning of a campaign, you can still succeed in the end. If you are challenged at the end, you will succeed if you started out on the best possible way. If you are threatened in the middle of a campaign, you succeed by starting well and finishing strong.

Adapting to Change Instantly

At each of the nine situations or stages covered in this volume, the general response is fairly simple but there are detailed key methods for executing each response. Again, to give you some context, we list those responses generally here.

- You avoid the dissipating stage by distracting critics by attacking them instead of defending yourself.
- During the easy stage, you cannot be satisfied with what is accomplished easily and work as hard as you can.
- During the contentious stage, you avoid getting into battles, and avoid competitors as much as possible.
- In the open stage, you keep up with your competitors and copy whatever they do.

- In the shared stage, you form partnerships, even with competitors.
- In the serious stage, you focus on generating rewards any way you can, even if only for the short term.
- In the difficult stage, you keep going, no matter how slow your progress becomes.
- In the limited stage, you must do the unexpected. You must get creative and unpredictable.
- In the desperate stage, you bring all your resources to bear as quickly as possible.

The faster you recognize and respond to these situations, the more certain your success becomes. You must respond to these situations automatically. This is only possible through drills and training. You want to act on instinct.. If you over-think these situations, you may question your judgment. This delays your response in a situation where you must act. The secret to success is making the right decisions quickly. The longer you delay, the less likely success becomes.

Controlling Expectations

To lead people, you must welcome challenges discussed in this volume. If you follow these rule, they give you an opportunity to show your abilities and win the confidence and support of others. People come together when they are threatened. This is a part of sharing a mission. People work together when they are in the same boat during a storm. When people share adversity, one person rescues the other just as naturally as the right hand helps the left.

This part of Sun Tzu's Playbook teaches us instant decision-making as the basis of confident leadership. You must recognize and explain the conditions you are in. You must know how to use each stage correctly. If you demonstrate that you know exactly what you are doing, you make it impossible for people not to trust you.

As a campaign continues, you must prepare people for situations becoming more difficult. Many of the principles in this volume cover the worst-case scenarios. A new position can stabilize and start producing rewards at any point in a campaign. If it does, great, but you need to prepare others for what may happen if it does not. When campaigns go perfectly, the situation takes care of itself. When they don't, you must take care of the situation. Few campaigns go perfectly from beginning to end.

Each stage of a campaign requires the appropriate reaction from others. Again, there are a lot of detailed key methods for preparing the expectations of others, but below we offer a general outline:

- To succeed in the dissipating stage, you need the commitment of others before a project begins.
- In the easy stage, you must let others know that you plan to go as far and as fast as you can. In the contentious stage, you use others to create obstacles for your competitors.
- In the open stage, you must get people to focus on your business, not your competitors.
- In the shared stage, you must get others to join you as partners.
- In the serious stage, you need to generate income from people in any way you can.
- In the difficult stage, you must give everyone a sense that you will not be discouraged.
- In the limited stage, you must make sure that your competitors do not know that you are vulnerable.
- In the desperate stage, you must prove yourself by putting an end to the crisis.

Your general goal in each situation is to make other people feel like they are winners for working with you. If you show them that you can respond to both blessings and difficulties, they will follow you. People will have no choice but to give you all they have. This is how you win their commitment.

Leverage Your Values

Your core mission acts as a stabilizing force as your new campaign passes through different stages and take you into different markets. The shared values defined by your mission unite you with others and give you strength. You must know to utilize this mission as you adapt to unexpected changes.

Your values cannot be just words and ideas. They must be part of the tangible value in your efforts. People must be proud of the value it puts in their products, services, and standards. If you use people's pride correctly, you will always beat the competition. Honesty and directness will always lend an advantage to your campaign. Your strength is built on trust and dependability.

Know When to Pause

Sun Tzu's Rulebook emphasizes that advancing a position requires resources. In any situation, you must have the resources to respond correctly. If you run low on resources, a response is impossible. This means you must know when to pause in an advance.

All people and organizations have temporary limits that restrict what they can do to meet their goals. You do not test these limitations. Leave yourself plenty of room for error. Give your ventures a margin of safety. You want to force your competitors to their limits. You must know and respect your own limitations. Your competitors can ignore their limitations. There is no need for you to make the same mistake.

Making great progress takes you into unknown areas. You don't want progress to trip you up. Problems can hide in the shadows of your business. A successful fashion can quickly become a worn-out fad. Your success can lead to confusion. You may not see that you are going against the changing trends. The confusion of markets can always surprise you. You must pause to reanalyze your market position. You never want to be surprised.

When your resources are stretched to the limit, you must develop more resources or do less . You must increase the size of your resources over time. To grow, you need to hold onto your current position and develop its resources. You shift from a competitive focus to a productive one.

6.0.0 Situation Response

Sun Tzu's eight key methods on selecting the actions most appropriate to a situation.

"You must develop these instant reflexes."
Sun Tzu's The Art of War 11:3:3

"When a warrior learns to stop the internal dialogue, everything becomes possible; the most far-fetched schemes become attainable. "
Carlos Castaneda

General Principle: We must drill ourselves to instantly recognize and respond to situations automatically.

Situation:

When we move to pursue an opportunity, we cross a critical threshold from simple decision-making to executing decisions. Sun Tzu called this movement "armed march" but we understand it more broadly as a competitive move or action. To pursue an opportunity, we must move into a region outside of our control. Once outside of controlled areas, we must respond instantly to the situations that we encounter. As important as reaction time is quickly deciding how to pursue opportunities, it is many times more important in responding to the immediate situations in which we find ourselves. Our range of potential actions collapses because the situation limits our options. If we don't know the best responses to these situations, we are going to get into serious trouble.

Opportunity:

Starting this new section, we move our discussion to the Move skills of Sun Tzu's Progress Cycle (1.8 Progress Cycle). Aim skills choose the highest probability opportunities (4.0 Leveraging Probability) and the best actions to explore them (5.0 Minimizing Mistakes). Move skills execute our aim decisions. Sun Tzu described in detail how they do this through situations response. These responses are required by situations that arise in the course of our move. There are nine classes of competitive situations that we encounter. Each of these classes has one best response. It gets even easier. While any of these classes of situations can arise in any move, they are most commonly found at certain stages of a competitive campaign.

Key Methods:

The following key methods guide the way that we respond to situation.

1. We must train ourselves to instantly recognize our situation. At this stage, the emphasis shifts from thought to action, from decision to execution. Our actions in a competitive environment are not executed like the steps in a plan. The job of making good strategic decisions gets more intense and demanding. We get information more quickly and we have to respond to it much more quickly as well (6.1 Situation Recognition).

2. We must also distinguish between simple moves and moves as a part of a larger campaign. A *campaign* describes longer term changes in position that consists of a sequence of moves. Campaigns are executed in smaller actions since smaller steps are more powerful. Within a campaign, we can recognize situations more easily because campaigns and the situations within them develop in a predictable, logical way (6.2 Campaigns).

3. Campaigns usually go through three stages. Each stage reveals more about the nature of the opportunity and has certain implications as far as creating situations. Understanding the stage of our campaign helps us better recognize the situation in which we find ourselves. Campaigns have beginning, middle, and end stages. Situations in each stage proceed logically from the nature of that stage (6.3 Campaign Patterns).

4. We must instantly separate competitive situations into one of the nine common classes. While every competitive situation has its unique characteristics, most fall into one of these nine categories. These nine situation classes are defined by differences in: 1) the true nature of the opportunity, 2) our position versus that of potential rivals, and 3) the depth of our commitment to the move (6.4 Nine Situations).

5. Once we recognize a situation, we must immediately know the one and only correct response. To reflect the fast pace of decision-making in making competitive moves, the best decisions are *responses* that arise from reflex rather than contemplation. Experience has demonstrated there is one, best response that works a high percentage of the time in each of the common situation. These responses have been proven over thousands of years of experience since they were first developed by Sun Tzu (6.5 Nine Responses).

6. We must pause our campaign when we run low on responses. The nine common situation responses are triggered by external developments. A growing lack of resources is an internal state that must also be monitored. While situation response requires us to focus externally on our situation, we cannot let ourselves lose sight of our internal need for resources (6.6 Campaign Pause).

7. Our dominant response must be tailored to three categories of unique characteristics. This is where the unique aspects of a position come into play. While our dominant response is dictated by standard situations, these same situations arise over and over again but they are never exactly the same. Every occurrence involves a unique constellation of conditions. We look at three categories of arena, relative size, and strength conditions *(*6.7 Special Conditions of Opposition).

8. Instant situation response creates key psychological advantages. By responding quickly and appropriately to challenging situations, we create confidence in our supporters and fear in our rivals. We improve the subjective dimensions of our position regardless of the objective rewards of our moves (6.8 Competitive Psychology).

Illustration:

The illustration that we usually use in our seminars to demonstrate these key aspects of situation response is a simple one of driving to the store to buy groceries. The decision that getting groceries is the best use of our time and that we are going to use a car are behind us. What happens when we get out on the road? This illustration makes solving these problems seem simple and indeed they are once we can apply them to every area of our competitive life as naturally as we do driving to the store.

1. We must train ourselves to instantly recognize our situation. If we don't run into problems, no responses are necessary. On this particular trip, we are going to run into problems. No strategic knowledge is necessary if we don't face challenges in our move. These key methods are for meeting challenges.

2. We must also distinguish between simple moves and moves as a part of a larger campaign. Let us assume that getting bread is part of a larger campaign of making special dinner for guests, which has certain deadlines.

3. Campaigns usually go through three stages. This is an early stage of a campaign, so we expect three potential situations and prepare mentally for them.

4. We must instantly separate competitive situations into one of the nine common classes. An early stage has three possibilities and let us assume we hit them all. An intrusion threatens to interrupt us before we get out the door. We initially find no problems on the road. Then we hit a serious traffic jam.

5. Once we recognize a situation, we must immediately know the one and only correct response. We must know to 1) evade the intruder, 2) not get distracted and go quickly on the open road, and 3) know how to get around the traffic.

6. We must pause our campaign when we run low on responses. Running low on gas after getting out the door? Don't ignore it and hope you don't hit more problems. We'll be in a world of hurt when we hit traffic. We stop and get gas.

7. Our dominant response must be tailored to three categories of unique characteristics. We have to adjust our responses depending on how far it is to the store, how big the traffic jam, and road conditions. For example, if the road is icy and slippery, we don't choose the same alternatives as we do when the roads are bare and dry.

8. Instant situation response creates key psychological advantages. By navigating the challenging road conditions, we become come confident that our dinner party will go well.

6.1.0 Situation Recognition

Sun Tzu's seven key methods on situation recognition in making advances.

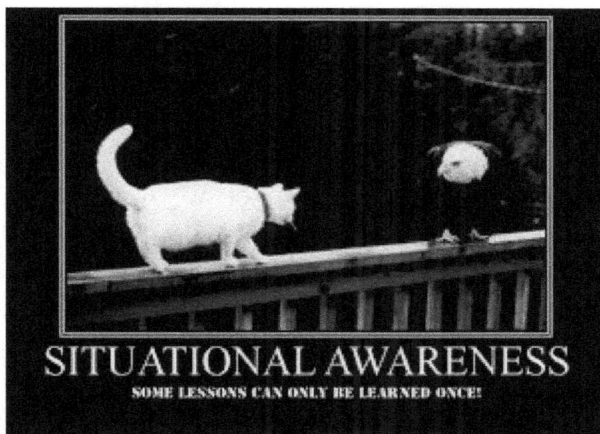

SITUATIONAL AWARENESS
SOME LESSONS CAN ONLY BE LEARNED ONCE!

"See the time to move.
Don't try to find something clever."
Sun Tzu's The Art of War 4:3:8-9

"Repetition of the same thought or physical action
develops into a habit which, repeated frequently enough,
becomes an automatic reflex."
Norman Vincent Peale

General Principle: Competition generates common classes of situations where we can know the appropriate response.

Situation:

Sun Tzu saw that every competitive situation had unique aspects. This diversity of conditions creates many problems for those trying to execute strategic decisions. The details of situations can easily confuse and distract us. Without a system for instantly recognizing different classes of competitive situations, we will often respond inappropriately. There are more than a thousand conditions important to competitive situations. Recognizing them all on a conscious level would be totally overwhelming. In situations where we must respond quickly and confidently, we cannot question every aspect of our situation.

Opportunity:

Another of Sun Tzu's common complementary opposites is the alternating use of expansion and contraction. When we look for opportunities, we expand our awareness. When we focus on pursuing one, we must know how to concentrate our efforts. If we can focus on the key elements distinguishing different classes of competitive situations, we can recognize the major categories of situations instantly. That recognition automatically triggers our situation response. We limit ourselves to recognizing the nine major classes of situations because we have techniques for drawing clear lines separating them (6.4 Nine Situations).

Key Methods:

The following warrior's key methods help us understand the nature and demands of situation recognition.

1. Competitive situations are event-driven changing relationships among competitors, rivals, and their environment. The triggering event is the pursuit of an opportunity. We cross a border from controlled territory to explore an opportunity. That event takes us into a new area and changes the relationship that we have with our rivals. This nature of relationship is what we call a situation (5.2 Opportunity Exploration).

2. As we get information more quickly, we must recognize situations instantly. In the course of making a move, the requirements of progress are more intense and demanding. Crossing a border puts us in immediate contact with new ground, potentially creating new rivalries. In listening and aiming phases of progress, time presses but it doesn't threaten to overwhelm. When we are executing a move, we are under much pressure to respond to conditions as they arise. In most situations, if we don't recognize what is happening almost instantly, the situation will quickly get out of control (6.1.1 Instant Reflexes).

3. Recognition must be geared to triggering a response. To reflect the faster pace, decisions at this stage are best understood as ***responses***. These responses arise from reflex rather than contemplation. Recognition of situations to which we do not know how to respond is worse than useless. Such recognition simply creates confusion. We focus on broad categories of recognition to eliminate gray areas and confusion, which are often even more destructive than the situation itself (6.0 Situation Response).

4. Recognition must be limited to relatively few generic situations. While we can pursue an infinite number of different types of opportunities using an infinite number of activities, recognizing situations requires a much narrower focus. While we could theoretically define a hundred generic situations and craft a hundred good responses to them, we could not execute them. The demands of time require us to limit our scope. We do so by limiting ourselves to recognizing those nine situations in which our instant response is critical to success. While limiting our focus to the nine most important situations is somewhat arbitrary, some limit is necessary, at least as a starting point. Over time, we can incrementally extend this list into more specific areas (5.0 Minimizing Mistakes).

5. Recognition must pick out key details to categorize a situation. The skill of situation response requires recognizing the key characteristics of situations. We must discern the difference between general conditions and the specific conditions that affect our responses. We cannot contemplate all conditions or even all relevant conditions. We must focus only on those dominant conditions which dictate the specific type of situation in which we find ourselves (6.1.2 Dominant Conditions).

6. Recognition must be unambiguous. We cannot know how to respond to ambiguous situations. Vacillation can not only eliminate our best option but create a more difficult situation. One of the key benefits of mastering the nine common situations is that they are unambiguous and exclusive. While other situations can arise out of our current situation, one situation always dominates our position (6.4 Nine Situations).

7. The skills of situation recognition can only be learned over time by practice. Situation recognition develops over time. This is true both in terms of our personal skills and in the course of a given move or campaign. We can adapt to situations correctly, sometimes without even recognizing them, but skill as situation recognition takes work to develop. While we can write and read about this situation, recognition is not an academic exercise. Our training programs are built around constant exercise in decision-making because it is only through those exercises that we can develop these types of skills. Our StrateSition Board Game was specifically designed around teaching the nine common situations and their responses in an environment based on building positions (1.8 Progress Cycle).

Illustration:

To put this idea in everyday terms, let us use the example of driving to the store to buy groceries (6.0 Situation Response).

1. Competitive situations are event-driven changing relationships among competitors, rivals, and their environment. The situation is the series of conditions we encounter on the road, culminating in a traffic jam.

2. As we get information more quickly, we must recognize situations instantly. The longer it takes us to recognize the formation of a traffic jam, the more likely it is that we will be trapped within it.

3. Recognition must be geared to triggering a response. If we are on a freeway and do not know the best response to the traffic jam, our recognition is useless.

4. Recognition must be limited to relatively few generic situations. Though traffic jams didn't arise until two thousand years after Sun Tzu, they fit nicely into his nine classes of situations.

5. Recognition must pick out key details to categorize a situation. To react appropriately to the traffic jam, we must know what the key differences are. In one type of situation, we can get off the freeway (6.4.3 Contentious Situations) while in another situation, when we are not near an exit, we must simply be patient (6.4.7 Difficult Situations). Both require very different responses.

6. Recognition must be unambiguous. Do we try to get off the road or should we be patient? Vacillation between the two on the road can lead to a worse situation, an accident.

7. The skills of situation recognition can only be learned over time by practice. Most new drivers are bad drivers simply because they lack the skills of situation recognition. What an experienced driver sees automatically from the signs, they miss entirely.

6.1.1 Conditioned Reflexes

Sun Tzu's four key methods on how we develop automatic, instantaneous responses.

"A daring soldier asks:
Can any army imitate these instant reflexes?"
We answer:
It can."

Sun Tzu's The Art of War 11:4:8-12

"It's all about hand-eye coordination, reflexes, timing,
strategy, being quick on your feet, being able to think
fast."

Johnathan Wendel

"The wise man does at once what the fool does at last."
Baltasar Gracian

General Principle: We can only develop instant reflexes through drill and practice.

Situation:

In making a move to advance our position, Sun Tzu taught that we are not executing a plan but exposing ourselves to events. The realm of strategy is the realm of uncontrolled events. We don't execute plans, but we still must think ahead and rehearse our possible responses. Sun Tzu taught that strategy demands more practice than production because we don't know what is coming next. Without practice, we cannot develop those instant reflexes. Our reflexes determines our success and failure. Without rehearsing our playbook, the more slowly we will react, and the less success we will have.

Opportunity:

Sun Tzu put together a detailed playbook. When asked if instant response were possible, Sun Tzu responded that they were a necessity. The faster we react correctly, the more successful we will be. Instant reflexes unite our seeing signs to situation recognition to knowing right responses to confident execution. This connection is only forged through practice. The research shows that the difference between experts and amateurs is simply in their depth of practice in developing instant reflexes. With more and more practice, we learn to pick out key conditions, connect them to situations, know their responses, and execute those responses automatically. An expert or master is simply one that is skilled at this.

Key Methods:

There are only four key methods we must follow to develop instant competitive reflexes.

1. We must practice recognizing key conditions instantly. We do not have time to analyze. Events are complex. Every event represents a unique combination of conditions. We do not have time to parse every aspect of every event. Even amid a chaotic, complexity of conditions, we can filter out all but the most important conditions in a given situation. We look for key condition in 1) the campaign stage, 2) the campaign class, 3) the form of ground, 4) the size of opposition, and 5) the strength of opposition (6.2.1 Dominant Conditions).

   2. We must practice instantly connecting key conditions to identify our situation. Once we recognize these key conditions, we must instantly know which situation we are in. Since situations have exclusive conditions, it should take absolutely no analysis to connect conditions to situations any more than it takes analysis to decide if nine is more than five (6.4 Nine Situations).

   3. We must practice instantly correlating the situation with its appropriate response. Each situation requires a single, known, definite response. The recognition of the situation and its response must be instantaneous. The beauty of instant reflexes is that, after we are trained, we don't have to reason our way to the right conclusion. We simply know it. We see the condition and respond without having to think (6.5 Nine Responses).

   4. We must practice the instant, skilled execution of responses. Knowing what to do is not the same as being able to do it. Execution requires practice. The more we practice, the more skillful we become. The human brain is malleable. It learns by doing. The more often we do something, or attempt to do something, the better we get at doing it. We progress from initial clumsiness to professional polish. Our goals should be to practice our responses to common strategic challenges until they become effortless. Our on-line training, especially our Warrior Class Lessons, are designed with that idea in mind. Only by continually challenging ourselves, can we develop the instant responses to conditions that situations require (5.6.2 Acting Now).

Illustration:

   An illustration from sports is the best here. Since this is being written in playoff season, let us consider American football.

   1. We must practice recognizing key conditions instantly. Though plays are learned from a book, recognition is learned on the field through practice. Players always know where they are on the field and what the down is. A player must pick out the few key tells that indicate what their opponent's play is going to be. Some, like the alignment of the players, happen before the play. Others, such as how hard the linemen block, actually happen during the play. Coaches drill their players in this recognition.

2. We must practice instantly connecting key conditions to identify a standard situation. As the play unfolds, the knowledge about down and distance connects with sound and movement. Sometimes, you can tell just by the sound of the blocking what is happening. To those who have played football, the sounds made when linemen try to create a passing pocket or open a running lane are very different sounds. Trained players instinctively recognize a running play or a passing play. They feel which way the play is flowing, indicating more specifics. Though football may have more or less than nine general classes of plays, players are able to distill the complexity to a handful of common situations, a run to the right, left, or middle, a screen pass, a short pass, pr a long-pass.

3. We must practice instantly correlating the situation with its appropriate response. Through practice, recognition of the situation immediately leads to recognition of personal responsibility. In a given situation, you know the man for which you are responsible or the lane for which you are responsible.

4. We must practice the instant, skilled execution of responses. Your feet start moving in the right direction in less than a second.

6.1.2 Prioritizing Conditions

Sun Tzu's six key methods for parsing complex competitive conditions into simple responses.

"Your first actions should deny victory to the enemy.
You pay attention to your enemy to find the way to win."
Sun Tzu's The Art of War 4:1:2-1

"Priority is a function of context."
Stephen R. Covey

"Control your own time. Don't let it be done for you. If
you are working off the in-box that is fed you, you are
probably working on the priority of others."
Donald Rumsfeld

General Principle: We tailor our response to five categories of conditions defining a situation.

Situation:

Underlying all of Sun Tzu's work is a respect for human limitations. A perfect system that is too complicated for most people to use is not really perfect at all. He saw that we are easily overwhelmed by the complex array of conditions that make up competitive situations. Different conditions suggest a variety of responses. Unfortunately, without training, most of us can easily come up with the wrong response because we lack the perspective on the overall objectives of the system.

Opportunity:

Situation response is Sun Tzu's play book. Along with it, he developed a systematic way of tailoring just the right kind of moves to fit a situation. In making a move, we are not executing a plan but navigating through the events that we encounter in the environment. We do this by immediately recognizing key conditions that suggest a single, specific response (6.1.1 Instant Reflexes). Assuming we never lose sight of our goals (6.2.2 Guidance by Goals), we need clear principles for prioritizing our responses from among a range of possibilities to make instant decisions.

Key Methods:

We can dramatically simplify the task of tailoring our responses to very specific conditions using the following key methods.

1. Five categories of conditions are the key to our situation. These categories of the conditions are:

- 1) the stage of our campaign (6.3 Campaign Patterns,
- 2) the nine situations or stages (6.4 Nine Situations),
- 3) the form of the situation we are in (6.7.1 Form Adjustments),
- 4) the relative size of our opposition (6.7.2 Size Adjustments), and

- 5) the relative strength of our opposition ([6.7.2 Size Adjustments](#)).

   2. Each category of conditions defines an exclusive aspect of a situation. In a given campaign, we can only be at one stage, in one common situation, on one form of situation, and meeting one opponent. The conditions within each category are exclusive. The campaign stage is either early, middle, or late. As the situation can be only in one of the nine common classes: dissipating, easy, etc. It occurs on only one form of various grounds: inclined, fluid, uncertain, or neutral. The opponent has only one size and strength even if it is an alliance of many separate individuals or groups. One situation can evolve into another as time goes on, but at any given point in time, we only respond to the specific situation that we currently face ([6.0 Situation Response](#)).

   3. The dominant response is dictated by the nine classes of situations. The campaign stage helps us understand which classes of situations are the most likely. After that, we use the characteristics of the situations themselves to parse them. Knowing the standard situation dictates the dominant response ([6.5 Nine Responses](#))

   4. The dominant response is adjusted to fit details of form and relative size and strength. We adjust our responses for the gravity, currents, or uncertainty of the ground. Our relative size and strength--or lack of it--determines how we adjust our responses against specific competitors when their presence shapes the situation ([6.7 Tailoring to Conditions](#)).

   5. If our response doesn't work as expected, we must spot where we went wrong and adapt. We are only human. As with every strategic endeavor, situation response is adaptive. If we get one part of the recognition wrong, we recognize our mistakes, learn of what parts are working, refine our actions, and try again ([1.9 Competition and Production](#).

   6. If we run out of resources, we must stop. Continuing beyond the limits of our responses is inherently dangerous, leading to almost certain defeat. ([6.6 Campaign Pause](#)).

Illustration:

To illustrate these key methods, let us imagine a specific business situation, a simple case study. Imagine you are in a meeting. In the meeting is a decision-maker, a person with all the authority and three people are working together against you. The topic under discussion is a critical business issue about which there is a disagreement. You take one side of the question and your rivals take another but they are not personally close. The decision-maker has shown no preferences on the question but his general character is well known to everyone in the meeting. The discussion is well-advanced and should be approaching a decision, but there are a number of difficult obstacles that must be worked through to arrive at that decision. There is a firm deadline for the meeting to end because the decision-maker is needed elsewhere.

Snap decision, what do you do?

1. Five categories of conditions are the key to our situation. Trained in Sun Tzu's system, we would instantly think about the stage, the nature of the situation, the form of the situation, and the size and unity of your opponents.

2. All five categories of conditions define exclusive aspects of situations. The campaign for decision is in a late stage. The situation is one defined by obstacles that slow progress. The form of the situation is dominated by a key single decision-maker. Opponents outnumber us but they are not tightly united.

3. The dominant response is dictated by the nine classes of situations. The stage and nature of the situation indicate that we are in a difficult situation. This situation requires persistence. Our primary focus must be on the obstacles not our opponents. We persistently work through those obstacles, taking our time rather than rushing.

4. The dominant response is adjusted to fit details of form and relative size and strength. The form of the situation is inclined, dominated by the decision-maker. We therefore slant our arguments to favor his or her known opinions and prejudices, especially try to position ourselves on his side against our opponents. Our opponents outnumber us, so we cannot attack them but they are not an over-whelming number so we can easily defend when they attack. However, they are divided so if they give you an opportunity, you work on their differences.

5. If our response doesn't work as expected, we must spot where we went wrong and adapt. We may see from the way the decision-maker reacts to something we said that we misunderstood his or her opinions. We immediately adjust our statements to fit our new understanding of his or her position.

6. If we run out of resources, we must stop. Though we are being persistent, when we come to the end of the meeting, we must stop.

6.2.0 Campaign Evaluation

Sun Tzu's five key methods on how we justify continued investment in an on-going campaign.

"Make war without a standard approach. Water has no consistent shape.
If you follow the enemy's shifts and changes, you can always find a way to win."

Sun Tzu's The Art of War 6:8:8-10

"I believe in the battle-whether it's the battle of a campaign or the battle of this office, which is a continuing battle."

Richard M. Nixon

General Principle: Campaigns must be evaluated in terms of length, mission, continuing cost and benefits.

Situation:

Campaigns involve a series of related moves toward a longer-term goal. Without understanding campaigns and the Playbook about their nature, we have a much more difficult time identifying and classifying the various competitive situations in which we find ourselves.

Opportunity:

Campaigns tie a group of related moves together (5.2.2 Campaign Methods). As a series of moves, campaigns have emergent properties that are not part of any given move (1.2.3 Position Complexity). The competitive situations in which we find ourselves are predictable because our movements have a history (1.1 Position Paths). Certain histories lead to certain types of development. Competitive positions interact in complex ways, but complexity can lead to order. We capture that order in our mental models to foresee situations (1.2.3 Position Complexity). Seeing campaigns as the frame for how and why situations develop is a simple and powerful tool.

Key Methods:

The following key methods describe the specific strategic challenges that commonly affect campaigns.

1. The longer time spans of campaigns permit more learning and more environmental change. In a dynamic environment, conditions continue to change throughout the course of a campaign. We learn more about the nature of the opportunity that we are pursuing. We inevitably discover barriers and problems that we didn't expect. Our position continues to change, changing its relative value to the position we are pursuing. New opportunities can arise that depreciate the benefits of the current campaign (1.1.1 Position Dynamics).

2. During a campaign we must not lose track of our larger mission. As we learn and conditions change, the original goal can lose its appeal, but we will still tend to continue the campaign because it has its own inertia. As campaigns continue, they, like all systems, can take on a life of their own. It is hard to get out of a campaign, even when the goal of the campaign no longer suits our purposes (1.6.2 Types of Motivations).

3. In campaigns, new investments must be evaluated only in terms of future returns not past investments. This rule applies to all actions, but it is especially important in evaluating campaigns. Campaigns last so much longer than most actions that they simply accumulate more sunk costs. In evaluating the benefits of well-defined and established positions, we must forget about past investments. We cannot change them. If we include them in our calculation, we will always over value the benefits of a campaign, throwing good money after bad. We cannot consider the benefits of a campaign without considering the value of learning more about the nature of the opportunity that they represent (5.4.2 Successful Mistakes).

4. The discovery of new opportunities must force us to reconsider an existing campaign. We must always consider the cost of not pursuing other opportunities. These costs are unavoidable if we stay the course of a campaign. These opportunity costs are built into every campaign in a way that makes them easy to overlook. Our environment can change well-defined and established positions into low-opportunity probability despite anything we do or fail to do. In moving, we can also discover new and better opportunities. If either of these conditions occur, we must make a conscious decision either to continue or abandon our campaign because other opportunities offer a better potential return on our time. We only have a limited amount of time and must invest it as wisely as possible despite being caught in a campaign (3.1.1 Resource Limitations).

5. We must never abandon a campaign simply because it becomes difficult. Campaigns typically go through a pattern where the penultimate stages are the most difficult. We must expect this going into a campaign. All campaigns are more difficult than we anticipated at first. We are always the most optimistic at the beginning of a campaign,. We don't discover the challenges until we get further into them. However, simply having more knowledge about the difficulties about a campaign alone cannot discourage us from continuing. We can never compare the known challenges in explored opportunities to the unknown challenges in unexplored opportunities. We must know exactly how to respond to the most common challenges. That way we are not frustrated by each new challenge ([6.3 Campaign Patterns](#)).

Illustration:

We have military campaigns, political campaigns, campaigns to find a job, and campaigns to graduate from college. While all face challenges, the campaign to get a college degree is one of the most commonly wasted.

1. The longer time spans of campaigns permit more learning and more environmental change. Fifty percent of college students change their major at least once and often several times. We must always be open to new conditions as they arise. Since I wanted to learn the law, during my first year as an undergraduate, I took a job doing legal research for a local legal firm.

2. During a campaign we must not lose track of our larger mission. While the law was academically interesting, from my work experience I found the actual practice of law a deadly bore.

3. In campaigns, new investments must be evaluated only in terms of future returns not past investments. Despite the past investment in a college education, I just didn't see continuing that investment, so I dropped out. I was already studying Sun Tzu and wanted to get into a more interesting competitive environment, one not so dominated by personal connections.

4. The discovery of new opportunities must force us to reconsider an existing campaign. I was also working in retail during summers and got promoted to a department manager. I had people with PHDs in political science and English literature working for me. At that point, I decided a business career simply made more sense. A better example of this, however, might be Bill Gates leaving Harvard to start Microsoft.

5. We must never abandon a campaign simply because it becomes difficult. For me, the easier thing would have been to stay in school. I had an academic scholarship. The academic work was easy and fun. I was also exposed to the emerging computer technology at Stanford, which was important to may later career.

6.2.1 Campaign Flow

Sun Tzu's six key methods for seeing campaigns as a series of situations that flow logically from one to another

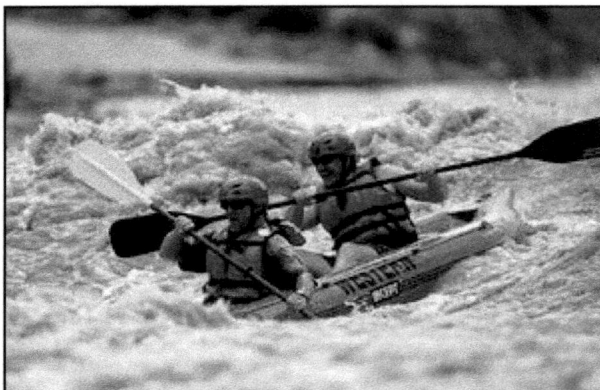

"Your war can take any shape.
It must avoid the strong and strike the weak.
Water follows the shape of the land that directs its flow.
Your forces follow the enemy, who determines how you
win."

Sun Tzu's The Art of War 6:8:1-7

"Take time to deliberate; but when the time for action
arrives, stop thinking and go in."

Andrew Jackson

"Reality is that which, when you stop believing in it,
doesn't go away."

Philip K. Dick

"We win some and we learn some."

Gary Gagliardi

General Principle: Control the flow of campaigns by leveraging the flow of one event into another.

Situation:

There are dangers in the flow of events during a campaign. Following Sun Tzu's logic, campaigns must accept the course of events and, at the same time, resist their course when they lead us into danger. To most of us, this appears to be a contradiction. This is because we don't understand how to use the balancing forces of complementary opposites. Guiding the course of a campaign is not like driving a car where our path is passive. It is like riding the rapids of a river. The path is turbulent with many hidden currents. We must both accept that turbulence and know how we can struggle against it.

Opportunity:

Sun Tzu taught that the flow of campaigns must be directed by the flow of events. Events create situations. The way we react to situations determines our success. Like riding a river, we use the flow of events to take us where we want to go. To do this, we must adjust from moment to moment to shifts in the current situation. We cannot simply follow the course of least resistance nor can we dictate the course of events. We shape our flow of actions in a campaign not by trying to control our environment but by mastering the skills of interacting with it (6.2 Campaign Evaluation).

Key Methods:

We master Sun Tzu's perspective for seeing competitive situations by remembering these five key methods.

1. Though we deal with events one at a time, it is best to think of them as a stream. Each action, especially responses to events, can have a distinct beginning and end, but they are not really separated. Each action and reaction flows from one situation to the next. In using Warrior's Playbook, we harness this perspective of flow as a part of our situation awareness. Situations are arising from nothing and returning to the void. They are flowing from one into the next, endlessly. Competitive landscapes are like kaleidoscopes where new situations are created from the reflections of the last (1.1 Position Paths).

2. We cannot control the natural flow of events during a campaign. An event is any action by any agent in our competitive landscape or any interaction of actions that creates unexpected conditions. Competitive landscapes are defined by the freedom of people to act in their own-self interest. This creates a steady stream of events that must be dealt with during a campaign (3.2.1 Environmental Dominance).

3. We cannot make progress if we fight against the flow of events. We must engage our environment. We cannot ignore events because they dictate our course as much as our own actions do. We cannot fight events because there are limits to our resources of energy and effort. There are no limit to the number of events that can affect the course of a campaign. (3.1.1 Resource Limitations).

4. We affect the flow of events by skilled responses to individual events. We don't have to respond to every event. When we do respond, we must do so because we recognize the best response. We leverage individual events in the flow of events. Our responses use the particular nature of a given event to our best advantage. We deflect events at the best angle to take us where we want to go. When people talk about "spinning" events, they are describing this process (2.3.1 Action and Reaction).

5. In reacting to the current event, we must be looking forward toward the next event. This means that we must be living in the moment. As we react, we are changing the situation but never decisively. Our actions are still a relatively small part of the environment. Most of our actions are quickly swallowed by the flow of events (1.2.1 Competitive Landscapes).

6. In a stream of events, the effects of our responses are cumulative. A single response to a single event never takes us exactly where we expect. We can recover from disasters as long as we survive. The turbulent nature of competitive environments come from the interaction of actions and reactions. As our responses interact with our environment, we discover what is needed for future moves. The course of a campaign is never straight, it is a result of the turbulence of events combined with our efforts to utilize them (1.9 Competition and Production).

Illustration:

Let us illustrate these principles in terms of a political campaign.

1. Though we deal with events one at a time, it is best to think of them as a stream. A candidate cannot get "stuck" on any one event during the campaign. A good campaigner takes both the good and bad in stride. The campaign moves on even if he or she doesn't.

2. We cannot control the natural flow of events during a campaign. The situations that can be controlled--rallies, mailings, ads-- are never as important as events in the environment--what political opponents do and say, economic and international crises, the breaking news, and so on.

3. t*We cannot make progress if we fight against the flow of events.* No matter how hard he or she works at controlling perceptions, a politician that isn't engaged with the flow of events is going to seem out-of-touch and disconnected. People will see these politicians as disconnected from the electorate, as though they are in a bubble.

4. We affect the flow of events by skilled responses to individual events. A skilled politician must know when and when not to respond to a rival's actions. For example, if a political rival makes a mistake, it is often best to let the media and the public dissect it rather than jump on the situation, getting directly involved.

5. In reacting to the current event, we must be looking forward toward the next event. In a sense, nothing is ever forgotten in a political contest. The politician who keeps moving forward creates a bigger impression than one that never lets go of one event and moves onto the next.

6. *In a stream of events, the effects of our responses are cumulative.* Winning an election depends on overall position. The politician that improves his or her position the most during a race is always going to be the one who responds the best to events during the campaign.

6.2.2 Campaign Goals

Sun Tzu's five key methods for assessing the value of a campaign by a larger mission.

"Methods shape systems to the authority of our mission."
Sun Tzu's The Art of War (Ancient Chinese Revealed version)
1:1:30-32

"If you don't know where you are going, any road will get you there."

Lewis Carroll

"I have found that great people do have in common an immense belief in themselves and in their mission."
Yousuf Karsh

General Principle: Campaigns are navigated by measuring progress toward our goals.

Situation:

Sun Tzu saw that campaigns can easily take on a life of their own. Since they cover long spans of time, months and even years, it is easy for us to lose sight of their ultimate purpose. This is especially difficult because campaigns involve more or less constant interaction with our environment. As we interact with our environment, it is easy to get turned around. As the flow of events take us in unanticipated directions, layer upon layer of short-term goals can eventually bury the original purpose of the campaign.

Opportunity:

Sun Tzu taught that the most important thing about the methods that we use is that they must be consistent with our mission (1.6 Mission Values). We must remember our mission not only in choosing how to explore an opportunity but throughout the entire series of activities we choose during the course of a campaign (5.1 Mission Priorities). Clarity of purpose is critical as we must react to what we find in the environment. For that to work, our values must be clear enough that we can never lose site of them.

Key Methods:

Let us contrast a couple of analogies to help us understand how we navigate our campaigns.

1. Every campaign has a larger mission than simply reaching the end. The goal of a campaign is to achieve a well-defined and established position, but that position is only valuable because it serves our larger mission. The problem is that campaigns continue for such a long time that simply finishing can become more important that the larger mission. This is why we must continually evaluate campaigns (6.2 Campaign Evaluation).

2. Our mission values provide a compass to keep our campaigns on track. A mission is more than a goal. It is a complete set of priorities. Those priorities include a set of values. Mission goals and values are not so much a restraint as a resource. As we are buffeted by events, only our values help us prioritize our often conflicting options. Clear values and outr need to make our values clear eliminate many choices that we would have to consider simply on the basis of completing the mission (6.2.2 Campaign Goals).

3. Our choice of methods during a campaign clarifies our mission values, making them more tangible. Values start as a guiding concept, but our choices during a campaign give them form and substance. The clearer our mission is, the more powerful it is. By putting our values into practice, they become more readily understood and shared by others 1.7.2 Goal Focus).

4. Campaigns create commitments to other people that impact our mission. One of the ways that missions take on a life of their own is that they involve commitments to other people. Honoring our commitments must be part of our values, but this potentially sets up a serious dilemma. When our mission values require us to abandon a campaign, we must sometimes find a way to honor our commitments outside of completing the campaign itself (1.6.3 Shifting Priorities).

5. We cannot let ourselves confuse satisfying our pride with satisfying our mission. Even when our mission is totally humanitarian and altruistic, it is based on our own personal interpretation on what is valuable to others. We can only base our goals and values on our unique, individual position, perspective, and consciousness. Because of this, it is very easy for us to confuse our mission with our personal pride. During the length of a campaign, we develop a natural pride of ownership over what we have achieved. It can be difficult to give up a mission that no longer serves our larger goals simply because of that pride. We must question all our decisions regarding mission to see if we are not confusing pride with mission (1.6.2 Types of Motivations).

Illustration:

Let us illustrate these principles with SOSI's campaign to build a comprehensive Sun Tzu's Playbook based on Sun Tzu's principles.

1. Every campaign has a larger mission than simply reaching the end. The Playbook is a means to an end. We want to make it must easier to learn and apply Sun Tzu's rich and complex competitive system.

2. ***Our mission values provide a compass to keep our campaigns on track.*** As each article of the Playbook is developed, we can measure it against the larger goal of making Sun Tzu's ideas more readily understood and broadly accepted.

3. ***Our choice of methods during a campaign clarifies our mission values, making them more tangible.*** We seek to provide concrete and tangible explanations and illustrations in the Playbook. They provide a practical standard against which people can evaluate the depth of their competitive knowledge and skill. Over time, we want to make the Playbook even more concrete by developing exercises in our training programs that illustrate the working so of these principles in simple forms of competition.

4. ***Campaigns create commitments to other people that impact our mission.*** Because of our commitment to publish an article on Sun Tzu's Playbook every day, we work to update and standardize our Playbook every day. At some point, our priorities will shift from developing articles to developing related training material. At that point, we may have to shift our commitments as well.

5. ***We cannot let ourselves confuse satisfying our pride with satisfying our mission.*** Our Rule Book is based on a conviction that mastering Sun Tzu's methods are important. These principles not only help people to become more successful individuals but a world trained in his system of "winning without conflict" will be less dangerous and wealthier in all senses of the word. Since creating the Playbook is a commitment that requires months and years, with no real compensation, there is a certain amount of ego involved, so I have to question whether this is really valuable to others or not and gladly solicit feedback.

6.3.0 Campaign Patterns

Sun Tzu's seven key methods on how knowing campaign stages gives us insight into our situation.

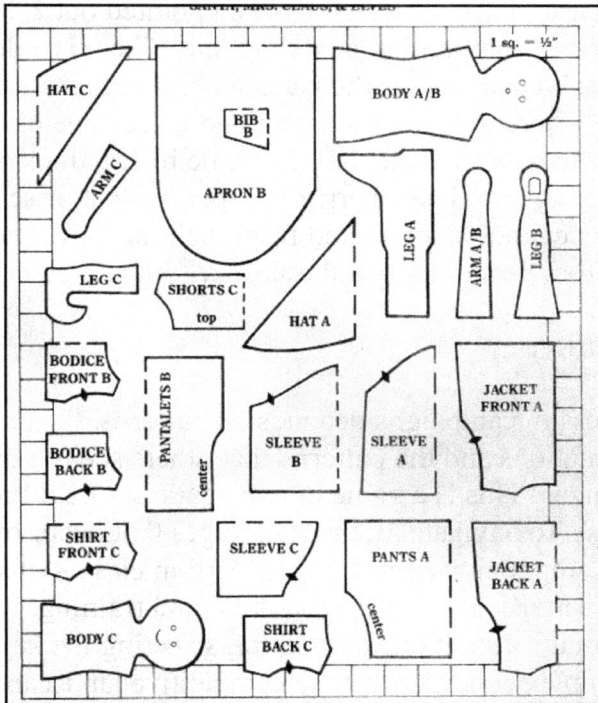

"You must control chaos.
This depends on your calculations."
Sun Tzu's The Art of War 5:4:10-11

"What we call chaos is just patterns we haven't
recognized. What we call random is just patterns
we can't decipher. What we can't understand we call
nonsense. What we can't read we call gibberish ."
Chuck Palahniuk

General Principle: Knowing what can happen in the course of a campaign is the key to controlling expectations.

Situation:

Through the course of a campaign, the competitive situations that arise appear chaotic, but, as Sun Tzu pointed out 2,500 years ago, the chaos of competition is not random. There is a deeper order underlying it. We cannot see the patterns in it because we haven't been trained where to look. Today we know this type of chaos as complexity, the patterns that arise from the interactions of independent, adaptive agents. The emergent properties that arise in these environments cannot be predicted from their elements, but we can learn them from observation and training.

Opportunity:

Our success in campaigns depends on patterns, the patterns that we see in situations and the patterns that others see in our handing those challenges. This is a game of expectations (7.2.2 Preparing Expectations). To navigate all the challenges that occur over the course of a campaign, we must expect certain classes of situations to arise in a pattern. Through preparation and training, we know which developing conditions to look for, selecting the key signs from the complex conditions of the competitive landscape (1.2.1 Competitive Landscapes). Most people cannot see these patterns, but they can see our pattern of reacting appropriately to them.

Key Methods:

The following eight key methods describe how we can use the stages of a campaign to determine our situation.

1. The confidence with which we handle challenges during the course of a campaign determines the depth of our support. The strength of competitive positions is determined by the strength of our support. Our supporters opinions form over time. While first impressions are important, the depth of our support can develop only over the course of a campaign, as others witness our handling of a series of challenges (1.7.1 Team Unity).

2. *In meeting challenges, we have an opportunity to demonstrate our ability to see what is hidden.* We handle situations with confidence when we know what to expect beforehand. Most people cannot see the same signs that we do, but they can see how easily we respond to different situations. Nothing increases confidence--our own or that of others--more than our ability to make successful predictions about how situations are likely to unfold. This same confidence and ability also discourages opposition from forming (3.2.2 Opportunity Invisibility).

3. *We see these patterns by knowing that campaigns usually go through three general stages.* At each stage, we can know what conditions to look for. From those conditions, we can know what class of situation we are in. From those situations, we can know how to respond. To help us understand the different stages that campaigns go through, we think of a campaign in terms of its beginning, middle, and end. By developing the appropriate conditioned reflexes to respond to each situation, we create an objective pattern of success others can observe (6.1.1 Conditioned Reflexes).

4. *These classes of situations don't only appear in campaigns, but it is more important to identify them when they do.* Campaigns require more investment and more support. When these situations arise in the pursuit of an ordinary opportunity, we lose that opportunity if we don't respond to them correctly, but when they arise in a campaign, the consequences of not handling them correctly are much more serious (6.2.2 Campaign Goals).

5. *We prepare ourselves and our supporters for the appropriate classes of situations at each stage of a campaign.* Of course, not every venture goes through all or even more of these situations or stages. A new venture *can* end successfully at any point in the process, running smoothly from start to finish. When things go smoothly, we don't have to worry about meeting these challenges. The point of this training is to prepare for situations that arise when our pursuit of a new position does not go smoothly (6.0 Situation Response).

6. The beginning stages arise when we cross our borders into new territory. This is the initial stage of discovery. In the initial stages, we first learn the basic position of potential rivals and the nature of the battleground, but the situations are relatively simple. The only difficult form of beginning stage is when we are forced to pursue a new position because our current position is directly threatened. Other than that, the easiest and most open stages of a campaign are when we first start to explore new territory (6.3.1 Early-Stage Situations).

7. In the middle stages, campaigns take on a deeper, more serious character. In these stages, competitors are more deeply committed, not only to exploring the territory but to a specific course of action. As we try to meet those challenges, three things happen. First, opportunities to develop significant advantages arise,. Second, resources get stretched more thinly. Third, your supporters can begin to waiver (6.3.2 Middle-Stage Situations).

8. The most difficult stages arise at the end of the campaign. If a campaign ends successfully before this point, all is well and good, but we have to be prepared for the problems that often arise at the end of many campaigns. At that point, we are totally committed to the success of a campaign and have fewer and fewer options. Our rivals are often in the same situation. In the end, the situation often gets desperate (6.3.3 Late-Stage Situations).

Illustration:

Let us illustrate these issues from the perspective of a project manager whose company has been hired to create and deliver a product, such as a software application, to a client company.

1. The confidence with which we handle challenges during the course of a campaign determines the depth of our support. As a project manager, everyone involved is looking to us for guidance. Those in our organization whom we control want to be protected from the customer from chaos so that they can get the work done. Those in the client organization are usually skeptical about the project simply because it represents change.

2. *In meeting challenges, we have an opportunity to demonstrate our ability to see what is hidden.* As the project goes forward, we are continually preparing the expectations of those involved. By letting them in on the potential problems that lie ahead, we are demonstrating that we are not approaching this project naively.

3. *We see these patterns by knowing that campaigns usually go through three general stages.* We should lay the potential issues out, both for our own people and our client's so that everyone knows what to expect. This can prevent problems and panic simply because everyone understands that we are prepared for what is likely to happen.

4. *These classes of situations don't only appear in campaigns, but it is more important to identify them when they do.* Because of the sunk costs involved, dealing with each subsequent situation becomes more important in terms of potential loss.

5. *We prepare ourselves and our supporters for the appropriate classes of situations at each stage of a campaign.* We should explain the three stages of a campaign, or in this case, a project. We assure everyone that we will make it clear which stage we are in and that each stage requires a change in response. This means that our priorities can change though the course of the project.

6. *The beginning stages arise when we cross our borders into new territory.* At the beginning, we should make it clear that the early stages, difficult or not, are the most transitory. Though challenges can arise at this stage, we can deal with them directly and quickly.

7. *In the middle stages, campaigns take on a deeper, more serious character.* As we arrive at this stage, we should again get everyone together and explain where we are. The issue is not just the project work that has gotten done, but the normal problems with integrating changes into the organization. We should explain specifically what class of situation we are encountering and what situations are the most likely to arise.

8. *The most difficult stages arise at the end of the campaign.* We should prepare everyone on both our side and the client's side for that stage from the beginning of the project. We should cast any terminal difficulties as a good sign rather than a bad one.

6.3.1 Early-Stage Situations

Sun Tzu's six key methods describing the common situations that arise the earliest in campaigns.

"Your first actions should deny victory to the enemy."
Sun Tzu's Art of War 4:1:23

"The ultimate wisdom which deals with beginnings, remains locked in a seed. There it lies, the simplest fact of the universe and at the same time the one which calls faith rather than reason."

Hal Borland

"Well begun is half done."

Aristotle

" ...a practical beginning, however small, for it is wonderful how often in such matters the mustard-seed germinates and roots itself."

Florence Nightingale

General Principle: The three early-stage situations arise from our most basic discoveries about conditions.

Situation:

Sun Tzu taught that there are three common situations that arise when we begin to explore an opportunity. These situations represent our most likely initial discoveries when exploring a new area. We might assume the entire campaign will assume the character of its earliest stages, but this perspective is simply wrong. Sun Tzu taught that the initial classes of conditions are the most temporary. Reacting inappropriately to these three situations and the campaign simply ends in failure. However, reacting correctly usually means that the current campaign stage evolves into a new situation.

Opportunity:

Beginnings are the most delicate times. Good responses at the initial stages of a campaign have more to do with preventing disaster than securing success. Bad decisions can lead to quick defeats that could have been avoided. On the other hand, good decisions at this juncture seldom lead to quick successes. Success comes from sustaining the campaign long enough to transform the initial stages of a campaign into another type of situation.

Key Methods:

The following key methods describe Sun Tzu's approach to handling the beginning of a campaign.

1. The initial situations in a campaign are defined by the discovery of basic conditions. Prior to undertaking a campaign, we observe from a distance. As we begin the campaign, we learn more about conditions by seeing the situation from the inside. We instantly learn the nature of the landscape and the disposition of our potential rivals. These two components define our initial situation (5.2 Opportunity Exploration).

2. These three classes of situations arise from the creation of a boundary situation. As we cross a boundary to explore an opportunity, we not only learn more, but we introduce ourselves into that the situation. We not only discover conditions, but our presence can change them. The nature of the opportunity has changed because of our presence. It will continue to change because others will respond to our presence (2.3.1 Action and Reaction).

3. The three initial classes of competitive situations are known as 1) dissipating, 2) easy, and 3) contentious. At the risk of terribly oversimplifying them, we can describe these three classes of situations fairly simply. Dissipating situations are those in which we are attacked. Easy situations are those where we make good progress. Contention situations are those where we meet immediate opposition (6.2 Campaign Evaluation).

4. Campaigns cannot be planned because, when we encounter these situations, we must respond appropriately. The situation is either invisible or doesn't exist until we cross the boundary to learn about it. We cannot plan our response. We are ignorant about what we will find. Hindsight bias leads us to think after the fact that these situations are more predictable than they really are. Good strategy starts with the assumption that we must react to events rather than plan them (5.2.1 Choosing Adaptability).

5. Initial campaign situations quickly evolve into more advanced situations. They can turn into other more advanced initial situations or they can turn into middle-stage or later-stage situations. Their order given by Sun Tzu, 1) dissipating, 2) easy, and then 3) contentious represents that standard order of development. Dissipating situations can turn into easy or contentious situations but the reverse is seldom true. Thus, recognizing our current situation not only helps us respond correctly to it, but we must be prepared for it to transform into something else, requiring instant reflexes (6.1.1 Conditioned Reflexes)

6. Middle-stage and late-stage situations cannot arise initially in campaigns because they need time to develop. Middle-stage situations can only arise from reactions to previous situations so we cannot start with them. Late-stage situations are so difficult and risky that they would be filtered out by any sensible process of choosing high probability opportunities (5.0 Minimizing Mistakes).

Illustration:

One way to understand these initial stages is to think about what can happen at the beginning of a plot of a science fiction movie.

1. The initial situations in a campaign are defined by the discovery of basic conditions. As the movie opens, we discover characters and the situations that they are in. In our science fiction movie, a space ship visits an alien world where sensors show that there are needed resources.

2. These three classes of situations arise from the creation of a boundary situation. The action starts once the exploration team goes down to the surface of the planet.

3. The three initial classes of competitive situations are known as 1) dissipating, 2) easy, and 3) contentious. There are only three possibilities. The explorers discover a big, dangerous alien horde already preparing to attack their ship or planet (dissipating situation). A non-threatening but alien environment that must be searched (easy situation). Aliens who are potential opponents (contentious situation).

4. Campaigns cannot be planned because, when we encounter these situations, we must respond appropriately. Our explorers could not have known which of these situations would occur until they began their exploration. They must react as situations develop.

5. Initial campaign situations quickly evolve into more advanced situations. What initially seems to be a non-threatening alien environment suddenly turns into contentious one when aliens are discovered.

6. *Middle-stage and late-stage situations cannot arise initially in campaigns because they need time to develop.* On a dramatic level, placing characters in the more complex middle-stage or late-stage situations is just confusing. Middle-stage situations arise from a series of actions and reactions, while believable characters wouldn't choose to go into the most series late-stage situation without some earlier reason to do so.

6.3.2 Middle-Stage Situations

Sun Tzu's six key methods on how progress creates transitional situations in campaigns.

*"Learn from the history of successful battles.
Victory goes to those who make winning easy."*
Sun Tzu's The Art of War 4:3:11-12

*"You don't develop courage by being happy in your
relationships everyday. You develop it by surviving
difficult times and challenging adversity."*

Epicurus

*"People who have lost relationships often wonder why
they can't just let it be "water under the bridge." It is
water under the bridge - the trouble is we do not live on*

the bridge but in the river of life with its many twists and turns."

Grant Fairley

"It seems essential, in relationships and all tasks, that we concentrate only on what is most significant and important."

Soren Kierkegaard

General Principle: Middle-stage situations arise from the different relationships created by different knowledge and resources.

Situation:

Sun Tzu's Warrior's Rulebook methods teach us that more is not just more but often different. This is especially true of the progress in a campaign. People often expect campaigns to continue as they began, but they never do. Situations do not just repeat themselves. They evolve over time. This means what works at the beginning of a campaign will stop working. Different situations require different responses. Certain situations arise as we become more deeply committed to an opportunity.

Opportunity:

These three situations all describe the condition of our relationship with others, specifically how relationships change as we get more deeply involved pursuing an opportunity. Our involvement in pursuing an opportunity cannot help but change our relationships with others. These situations include relationships with our rivals and supporters and illustrate how easily those roles can change. While it seems like relationships can develop in an infinite number of directions, there are only three directions that are common.

Key Methods:

The following key methods explain the situations that develop in the middle of a campaign.

1. The middle situations in a campaign are defined by the evolution of relationships. This evolution is not driven by personality. It is driven by the nature of the ground and the nature of the opportunity. As time goes on, we learn more about the nature of the competitive landscape. Middlestage situations arise directly from that knowledge (1.2.1 Competitive Landscapes).

2. These three classes of situations require a deeper commitment to the campaign. We only progress to the middle stages if the campaign isn't an instant success or instant failure. We must discover enough promise that we want to continue and problems that require more work. To continue, the project requires more commitment. The nature of that commitment is what separates these different situations (2.3.3 Likely Reactions).

3. The middle three classes of competitive situations are known as 1) open, 2) intersecting, and 3) serious. Though it oversimplifies them, let us offer some simple descriptions of these three situations. An open situation is a race that isn't determined by speed. An intersecting situation is a joining of forces. A serious situation is a cut-off of resources that is determined by lack of support. (6.2 Campaign Evaluation).

4. We must know instantly how to react when we get into these situations. These situations arise because everyone involved must adapt to the situation. We cannot plan our response, but we can know how to respond. We must react appropriately from instinct rather than doing what we want (5.2.1 Choosing Adaptability).

5. Middle campaign situations evolve more slowly into other middle-stage or end-stage situations. The challenges represented by middle-stages are deeper, representing our deeper knowledge of the situation. This means that they take more time to resolve, evolving more slowly. Open situations can develop into intersecting situations, but serious situations are a wild-card, arising at any time (6.1.1 Conditioned Reflexes).

6. *Middle-stage situations are all concerned with resource management*. Because this situation takes time to evolve and more time to resolve, they focus in different ways on getting the most

return possible from what the situation offers (3.1.1 Resource Limitations).

Illustration:

Let us think about these situations from the perspective of managing a professional sports team through a long season.

1. The middle-stage situations in a campaign are defined by the evolution of relationships. Over the course of the season, the relationship among the various teams vying for the title develops gradually.

2. These three classes of situations require a deeper commitment to the campaign. While teams can switch players around at the beginning and end of seasons, the middle stages reflect a commitment to a given lineup of players.

3. The middle three classes of competitive situations are known as 1) open, 2) intersecting, and 3) serious. Teams at the top of their division tend to be in an open situation. Those in the middle tend to be in an intersecting situation. Those at the bottom tend to be in a serious situation.

4. We must know instantly how to react when we get into these situations. Their positions in team standing are not certain because they change every week. A team at the bottom of the standings can rise. A team at the top can fall. Everything depends on them reacting appropriately to their current situation.

5. Middle campaign situations evolve more slowly into other middle-stage or end-stage situations. Team situations can change dramatically between the middle of the season and the end, but those changes will go much more slowly than at the beginning or the end.

6. M*iddle-stage campaign situations are all concerned with resource management*. Professional players play a long season. They must know how to make the most of their resources given their particular situation.

6.3.3 Late-Stage Situations

Sun Tzu's six key methods for understanding the final and most dangerous stages of campaigns.

"Avoid the enemy's high spirits.
Strike when his men are lazy and want to go home.
This is how you master energy."

Sun Tzu's The Art of War, 7:5:7-9

"Though no one can go back and make a brand new start, anyone can start from now and make a brand new ending."

Carl Bard

"It is better to spend one day contemplating the birth and death of all things than a hundred years never contemplating beginnings and endings."

Buddha

> *"If you want a happy ending, that depends, of course, on where you stop your story."*
>
> Orson Welles

General Principle: Final stage situations are always the most challenging.

Situation:

These final situations are the most difficult challenges the we face in the course of a campaign. They are the riskiest, with the highest probability of loss. We would prefer to conclude our campaigns without passing through these stages. Unfortunately, experience teaches that few things of value are won easily.

Opportunity:

If a campaign ends prior to these final stages, we obviously avoid their worst-case scenarios. All of our earlier decisions attempt to avoid them. Unfortunately, no matter how we tip the odds in our favor, strategy is a probabilistic process. That means that there is always a chance we will find ourselves in the most challenging situations (1.8.4 Probabilistic Process). Actually, given enough campaigns, it is only a matter of time. If we are wise, we train for these worst case scenarios. Because of their danger, we must understand them more clearly than all other situations. Recognizing and knowing how to respond to them is literally a matter of life and death. Responding to these situations correctly provides us with the greatest upside, saving ourselves from complete disaster.

Key Methods:

The following key methods explain the challenges of late-stage situations.

1. These final three classes of situations are the most difficult and dangerous. We do not get to this stages if our campaign is successful. Because these situations are the most challenging, the mistakes we make during them are the most costly. Since mistakes are so costly, knowing the right responses is valuable (5.0 Minimizing Mistakes).

2. The final three classes of competitive situations are known as 1) difficult, 2) limited, and 3) desperate. Though it oversimplifies them, let us offer some simple descriptions of these three situations. Difficult situations encounter obstacles that slow progress. Limited situations describe a transition that must be made secretly. Desperate situations are do-or-die situations where our goal is survival (8.7.2 Abandoning Positions).

3. We run into these situations when our goal is near. The proximity of our goal makes going through these situations worthwhile. By resolving these final stage problems, we can claim the rewards offered by the entire campaign (8.0 Winning Rewards

4. Failure is certain if we do not know how to react to these situations. These three situations all describe different types of problems that must be resolved before a campaign can be concluded. Missteps are easy. Each requires us to do something that is against our instinct (5.2.1 Choosing Adaptability).

5. Late-stage campaign situations require the right character. They all certainly require courage and confidence, but character plays a more subtle role involved with timing. The response to each of these situations requires a certainty about how we can use time in our favor (1.5.1 Command Leadership)

6. Improperly handled, one of these situations can easily lead to another. These situations can form a kind of chain reaction. Slower progress can be followed by a difficult choice, which itself can be followed by a desperate situation. Needless to say, Sun Tzu's principles of response are designed to avoid these situations whenever possible, but even then, there is a potential connection. All we can do is cope in the best way possible with what the environment gives us (3.2.1 Environmental Dominance).

Illustration:

Think of these stages as arising when fighting a fire.

1. These final three classes of situations are the most difficult and dangerous. If everyone gets out of the building and the fire gets put out, no problem. However, the longer the fire fight goes on, as long as people are trapped, the more likely these situations are to arise.

2. The final three classes of competitive situations are known as 1) difficult, 2) limited, and 3) desperate. The fire is persistent. We save someone from a tight situation taking a risk. We are trapped by the flames.

3. We run into these situations when our goal is near. The last person saved is always in the most serious situation.

4. Failure is certain if we do not know how to react to these situations. People will die.

5. Late-stage campaign situations require the right character. We cannot be panicked into rushing or frightened into going too slow.

6. Improperly handled, one of these situations can easily lead to another. The hard to put out fire will turn into a life-or-death situation.

6.4.0 Nine Situations

Sun Tzu's ten key methods defining the nine common competitive situations.

"A commander provides what is needed now.
This is like climbing high and being willing to kick away
your ladder.
You must be able to lead your men deeply into different
surrounding territory.
And yet, you can discover the opportunity to win."
Sun Tzu's The Art of War 11:5:12-15

"It is a challenge. I spoke about things being
uncomfortable sometimes. It's not always going to be a
situation where it's going to be convenient for you."
Rubin Carter

General Principle: Before responding to a situation, we must know its general nature.

Situation:

Sun Tzu's system recognizes that competitive situations are complex and constantly changing. As we pursue opportunities, our progress itself naturally changes our situation. Every situation is unique, but they have characteristics in common. Situations occur on the similar forms of ground. Our rivals can take certain types of positions against us. Our commitment to the venture can vary. Still, none of these conditions always dictate the same response. Our response depends on the larger situation in which we find ourselves.

Opportunity:

The secret is in knowing how situations combine these characteristics. Sun Tzu's Playbook defines nine common classes of situations. These classes combine different types of ground, opposing postures, and levels of commitment. The power of recognizing these situations is that each has one and only one correct response. When we recognize the situations, we know exactly what to do. When a situation doesn't meet the situations criteria, we know what not to do. Our skills at situation response depend upon instant recognition of these situations.

Key Methods:

We list these nine common classes of situations below to give a basic understanding of what they are and how they develop naturally out of the current situation. Any situation can arise with any move and usually many will arise during the course of a campaign.

1. The nine classes of situations both qualify and disqualify a given situation from a given response. These classes of situations provide templates for action. As we will see, the definitions of these situations get very specific. These specifics are important. If a situation does not meet all the specific conditions of its type, the missing conditions point to the proper response (6.5 Nine Responses).

2. We are sometimes forced to find an opportunity because our existing position is threatened. In a lesser form, this situation takes the form of natural pressure against pursuing a new venture as an opportunity, but in its specific form, something more is required. We call this a dissipating situation (6.4.1 Dissipating Situations).

3. Campaigns get off to an easy start as we stay close to what we know. Frequently just the novelty of getting into a new territory gives us certain advantages. This is an easy situation (6.4.2 Easy Situations).

4. If a new opportunity is very appealing, other competitors and rivals will discover it as well. Sometimes, our initial success in the opportunity gives them the idea. This is a contentious situation (6.4.3 Contentious Situations).

5. We and our opponents can make quick progress along different routes without conflict. We can build our position while competitors can also build their positions in different ways. This is an open situation (6.4.4 Open Situations).

6. Over time, we and potential rivals pursue an opportunity along the same lines. None of us have all the skills and resources needed to establish a dominant position. These different groups bring different forms of value to create a complete solution. This is a intersecting situation (6.4.5 Intersecting Situations).

7. Our investment to establish our position gets larger and larger. At this point, even our supporters can become critics of the new venture, threatening to cut off funding. This is a serious situation (6.4.6 Serious Situations).

8. As we explore the opportunity more deeply, we discover barriers that slow progress. We must overcome these barriers to make the venture successful. This is a difficult situation (6.4.7 Difficult Situations).

9. When a move gets close to a conclusion, we reach a key transition point. During this time, our options are severely limited. The transition is delicate and can be derailed if opposition arises. This is a limited situation (6.4.8 Limited Situations).

10. As we get to the very end of the campaign, we can succeed only if we commit all our resources. We must do this quickly because our venture will fail if we delay. This is a desperate situation (6.4.9 Desperate Situations).

Illustration:

Let us illustrate these ideas with a scenario about starting a business as a hairdresser as a friend of ours once did have quitting a big salon.

1. The nine classes of situations both qualify and disqualify a given situation from a given response. Going into a new business, the new owner doesn't know what situations he or she will encounter but must pick the best responses and avoid damaging ones in order to survive, given that 80% of new businesses do not survive.

2. Sometimes we are forced to pursue any new opportunity because our existing position is threatened. We must start our own business because we lost our job and cannot find a new one. In this example, let us say that we are a hairdresser.

3. Campaigns get off to an easy start as we stay close to what we know. We start a business using our existing skills by making contact with our existing customers and offering to visit them in their homes to do their hair.

4. If a new opportunity is very appealing, other competitors and rivals will discover it as well. Our "at-home" service is very popular, so we start working with other hairdressers who work as freelancers. Some of the hairdressers start their own competing businesses. "At home" service is popular. It attracts other hair-dressers and salons into offering it.

5. We and our opponents can make quick progress along different routes without conflict. There are a lot of different types of customers in different areas of town so direct competition is limited. Different at home providers concentrate on different groups of customers and types of services-coloring, perms, etc.

6. Over time, we and potential rivals pursue an opportunity along the same lines. As our business grows, we spread out through town and expand our services. Other successful organizations do as well. We start having problems with consistent standards and quality from our free-lance work force.

7. Our investment to establish our position gets larger and larger. Since we have been growing so quickly, we have had to borrow money from the bank. However, despite our growth, we don't seem to be making a profit and the bank cuts us off.

8. As we explore the opportunity more deeply, we discover barriers that slow progress. In making the transition from a hairdresser to a business owner, we are forced to master a whole new set of management skills.

9. When a move gets close to a conclusion, we reach a key transition point. The market has reached a saturation point and poor management has forced us to change our original model. We are going to change from using free-lancers to hiring and training our own hairdressers who are employees, but the transition will take time.

10. As we get to the very end of the campaign, we can succeed only if we commit all our resources. Our free lancers revolt against the transition, starting their own competing organization. We must respond quickly or lose everything.

6.4.1 Dissipating Situations

Sun Tzu's five key methods on situations where defensive unity is destroyed.

"Warring parties must sometimes fight inside their own territory.
This is scattering terrain."
Sun Tzu's The Art of War 11:1:11-12

"Divide and rule, the politician cries; unite and lead, is watchword of the wise."
Johann Wolfgang von Goethe

"Words divide us, actions unite us."
Tupamoros Slogan

General Principle: Dissipating situations arise when defensive unity is clearly threatened by an attack.

Situation:

A competitor or rival is mounting a large, well-organized attack on our existing position. Given its size and power, this invasion is very likely to be successful. At the very least, the confrontation with this opponent will be difficult and expensive. We are forced to defend our existing position within our own territories. The main problem here is not the rival, but the internal division that the threat causes.

Opportunity:

This is called a dissipating situation because it dissipates our strength. In Sun Tzu's system, strength comes from unity (1.7 Competitive Power) , especially in defense (1.7.1 Team Unity). Joining with others doesn't mean that we all don't have our separate interests. It measn that our shared mission is more important and more defensible (1.6.1 Shared Mission).

Key Methods:

We use the following principles to clearly identify the conditions that create a dissipating situation.

1. An opponent forces us into the campaign by creating a dissipating situation. A dissipating situation arises at the beginning of a campaign because the situation creates the campaign. We do not create these situations ourselves, at least not by our choice of immediate actions. These events are outside of our control (3.2.1 Environmental Dominance).

2. In a dissipating situation, the attacking force must be large enough that we cannot defend our existing position. Since it is easier to defend than attack, the attacking force must be so large that we cannot defend against it. Given the principles of force size, the force must be many times larger than our defending force (6.7.2 Size Adjustments).

3. In a dissipating situation, the attacking force must be well-organized. This means that there are no internal divisions within the group attacking us. If these internal fractures exist, we should attempt to divide the force to reduce it to a size against which we can defend (9.2.5 Organizational Risk).

4. In a dissipating situation, the attack must be on our territory, on our span of control, rather than on our competitive forces. The attempt must be to take away our existing position not simply undermining our attempts to win a new position. Since we are being attacked in our own territory, we cannot evade the larger force by the principles of force size (5.6.1 Defense Priority).

5. Because the threat is to our existing position, our supporters are likely to abandon us in a dissipating situation. While they may support our position, they are more concerned with maintaining their own positions. In other situations, they might normally support us, but under the nature of the threat here, most will likely desert us to protect themselves. They put a higher priority on defending themselves than on helping defend our position (1.6.3 Shifting Priorities).

Illustration:

Let us illustrate these key methods with a case study where a large, well-known company announces that it is targeting a market niche that is occupied by a much smaller, local company.

1. An opponent forces us into the campaign by creating a dissipating situation. No actions at the smaller company could have avoided triggering this event. Indeed, it is the success of the small company's position that attracted the tact.

2. The attacking force must be large enough that we cannot defend our existing position. The large, well-known company moving "down market" sets aside an overwhelming amount of resources and money given the size of the market.

*3. **The attacking force must be well-organized.*** There is no internal conflict created by their decision to go after the smaller company's market.

*4. **The attack must be on our territory, on our span of control, rather than on our competitive forces***. The large company is not simply trying to take away new customers, they are specifically targeting the smaller company's existing customers, trying to take them away.

*5. **Because the threat is to our existing position, our supporters are likely to abandon us.*** In this case, supporters include the smaller company's existing employees, service providers, suppliers, and their customers. This attack throws people into chaos. Employees start looking for jobs elsewhere, possibly with the invader. Customers and suppliers who have worked with the smaller company for years are suddenly divided. Each is concerned about how the change will affect their particular positions.

6.4.2 Easy Situations

Sun Tzu's five key methods for recognizing situations of easy initial progress. .

"When you enter hostile territory, your penetration is shallow.
This is easy terrain."

Sun Tzu's The Art of War 11:1:13-14

"Almost everything in life is easier to get into than out of."

Anonymous

"There's no thrill in easy sailing when the skies are clear and blue, there's no joy in merely doing things which any one can do. But there is some satisfaction that is mighty sweet to take, when you reach a destination that you thought you'd never make."

Spirella

General Principle: Easy situations sow the seeds of future difficulties.

Situation:

The "easy situation" arises when we first begin a move or a campaign and have a minimal commitment to it. It defines a situation where we can seemingly make progress easily. As a result, we form our expectations regarding the future of the move. The problem is both our lack of commitment and a set expectations based on minimal experience. Without making a commitment, it is easy to get distracted. Our set of expectations are almost certainly wrong.

Opportunity:

Our perception of progress comes from our expectations compared to reality (1.3.1 Competitive Comparison). Before making a move or starting a new campaign, we usually have a number of concerns and worries. As we begin to actually act, there is a kind of relief of pressure. We often discover that many of our concerns were unwarranted. When this happens, it is a tremendous opportunity if we know how to take advantage of it, but because of the special nature of our easy situation, we often do not.

Key Methods:

The kyey methods for identifying an easy situation are:

1. An easy situation can occur only at the beginning of a move or campaign. Other situations can resemble an easy situation because they lack significant barriers, but the ease of an easy situation is of a special kind. It is easy both in the sense of representing few significant barriers but also easy in the sense that it causes no real concern (6.3.1 Early-Stage Situations).

2. In an easy situation, we lack commitment because the move or campaign is just beginning. The more we invest in a move or campaign, the more committed we become to making it work. Though sunk costs should not influence our commitment to pursuing an opportunity, the fact is that they often do (6.2 Campaign Evaluation).

3. In an easy situation, we have no challenges that slow us. When we stay close to what we know, as we are at the beginning of all moves, we make quick progress, both in learning and in physically moving. This easy initial progress is easy to take for granted. Only as our distance from our current position increases, do we usually encounter the challenges of establishing a new position (4.4 Strategic Distance).

4. In an easy situation, we are easily distracted because of our lack commitment. This is the second, perhaps more important sense in which these situations are easy. Easy progress is easy to take for granted. Our choice of pursuing a given opportunity is made moment-to-moment. Since the easy situation arises early in a campaign, before we have made any significant commitment to the opportunity or been engaged by any serious challenges, events can easily distract us from them (5.1.1 Event Pressure).

5. The easy situation sows the seeds for its own future difficulties. Most campaigns that are easy at first naturally grow more difficult over time. We are easily distracted in an easy situation. We think that we will continue making easy progress even if we take a break to do something else more pressing. We always think that the opportunity represented by an easy situation will keep. But our fast progress will naturally create opposition. We are mistaken if we think of an easy situation as friendly territory. The easy situation leaves us poorly prepared to these situations as they naturally reverse themselves (3.2.4 Emptiness and Fullness).

Illustration:

A group is given the task of designing a product for a specific market. The product development deadline is three months away at the beginning of the project.

1. An easy situation can occur only at the beginning of a move or campaign. Once the analysis is finished and the group starts working, the product comes together quickly. After a week, the project seems about half done. What could go wrong?

2. Because the move or campaign is just beginning, we lack commitment to it. Management is happy with the progress, but since things are going so well, the energies are naturally focused elsewhere.

3. We often meet no challenges that slow us at the earliest parts of a move. At this point, the project seems trivial. People are not losing sleep over it. They look at their schedule and the project and feel only complacency.

4. Because of our lack of commitment, we are easily distracted in these situations. Since the project is so far ahead of schedule, it is easy to pull people off of it when other needs naturally arise. Even if management doesn't do this, people find it much easier to put their time into personal matters since the project seems well in hand.

5. The easy situation sows the seeds for its own future difficulties. Time passes and deadlines grow nearer when the inevitable problems and barriers are encountered. There is much less time and resources to address those problems because of the project's initial easy situation.

6.4.3 Contentious Situations

Sun Tzu's four key methods for identifying situations that invite conflict.

"Some terrain gives you an advantageous position. But it gives others an advantageous position as well.
This will be disputed terrain."
Sun Tzu's The Art of War 11:1:15-17

"The well-meaning contention that all ideas have equal merit seems to me little different from the disastrous contention that no ideas have any merit."
Carl Sagan

"Such democracies have ever been spectacles of turbulence and contention; have ever been found incompatible with personal security or the rights of property; and have in general been as short in their lives as they have been violent in their deaths."
James Madison

General Principle: Contentious situations offer obvious rewards that tempt people into conflict.

Situation:

The contentious situation arises when we discover that an opportunity is very rewarding, but others discover it as well. Because of an opportunity's obvious potential, it attracts competitors. The opportunity initially looks like an opening, but because others react to it as we have, the opening is not closed but it is contested. While no one has yet established a position taking advantage of the opening, there are a number of competitors vying to do so.

Opportunity:

The contentious situation arises because the opportunity's abundant benefits seem equally available to all contenders. None of them have established positions. If the benefits were not abundant, it would be easy to leave the opportunity because of its potential for conflict. Unfortunately, the benefits are real. Big opportunities are rare, hence, the strategic problem (4.0 Leveraging Probability).

Key Methods:

The following principles identify the conditions of a contentious situation.

1. In a contentious situation, the area of opportunity quickly demonstrates that it offers rewards or advantages. If there were no rewards, there would be no basis for contention. If the rewards were not fairly obvious fairly quickly, the area would not draw adversaries into contention (8.0 Winning Rewards

2. In a contentious situation, the extent of the rewards and the costs of harvesting them are unknown. Since this is an early-stage situation, those involved have not had time to learn the deeper nature of the territory. As more is learned, different non-conflicting paths or ways to share in the benefits of the territory may be discovered (2.1.1 Information Limits]).

3. In a contentious situation, those rewards seem equally available to all of those pursuing them. In other words, no one has control of them and no one has a clear advantage in getting control of them. Conflict is usually avoided by someone demonstrating a superior position. In a contention situation, no one has had time to develop such a position (6.3.1 Early-Stage Situations).

4. The contentious situation tempts those vying for the opportunity to fight each other over it. No one wants to leave the field of competition because of the potential that it offers. Those involved focus on the rewards of the situation, which are readily apparent, rather than the costs of conflict, which are not (3.1.3 Conflict Cost).

Illustration:

A great example of a contentious situation is the early stages of a presidential campaign where a number of candidates are still in contention for their party's nomination.

1. The area or opportunity being explored quickly demonstrates that it offers rewards or advantages. The advantage of a nomination for the president are well known.

2. The extent of the rewards and any restrictions on harvesting them are not yet known. Early in the campaign, before the primaries, the candidates do not know which of them will draw the most votes or even the most funds in the contest.

3. Those rewards seem equally available to all of those pursuing them. All the candidates see themselves as positioned equally in terms of winning the contributions of supporters and the votes of primary voters.

4. This contentious situation tempts those vying for the opportunity to fight each other over it. The candidates naturally meet to debate the issues, setting up a situation where they are encouraged to fight it out. As Sun Tzu predicts, this fight weakens all candidates so that, when running against an incumbent, the challenger seldom wins.

6.4.4 Open Situations

Sun Tzu's five key methods for recognizing situations of that are races without a course.

"You can use some terrain to advance easily. Others can advance along with you.
This is open terrain."
Sun Tzu's The Art of War 11:1:18-20

"Plodding wins the race."
Aesop

"The trouble with the rat-race is that even if you win, you're still a rat."
Lily Tomlin

General Principle: Open situations create a race without a clear route.

Situation:

The challenge in an open situation is finding the best way to utilize a given opportunity. The open situation puts us in a contest where the best methods for winning the contest are uncertain because they depend upon the as-yet-unknown potential of the ground. We are forced to choose among alternative routes with the clear probability of choosing the wrong such path.

Opportunity:

There are two opportunities for learning in an open situation. One is to learn more about the nature of the ground and how to secure its benefits. The second is to learn from our rivals, by observing their progress along the paths that they have chosen.

Key Methods:

We use the following mehods to clearly identify when we are in an open situation.

1. A open situation occurs only in the middle of a campaign. In a sense, it defines the conditions that separate the beginning of a campaign from its middle. It is based on a deeper but incomplete understanding of an opportunity. In the beginning of a campaign, our understanding and that of our rivals, isn't deep enough to create an open situation. At the end of a campaign, that understanding is more complete and positions have solidified to a degree to close off an open situation (6.3.2 MiddleStage Situations).

2. In an open situation, competitors have different options about how to pursue the opportunity. Our situation is uncertain in terms of which direction will yield the best results. There are alternative paths and methods that can be used to establish a position on the basis of the same opportunity. The best route depends upon the still evolving nature of the situation, that is, what others do, and the deeper nature of the environment, which remains to be discovered (3.2.1 Environmental Dominance).

3. In an open situation, there is a race among competitors to discover the complete solution. Not everyone will end up with a winning position. We may be ahead in some aspects of developing a position, but we may be behind in others. The challenge is to be among the first competitors to discover the right formula for a complete and productive position (1.3.1 Competitive Comparison).

4. In an open situation, competitors are making different types of progress by using different methods. No single, superior path toward success has yet been identified. Such a single path may or may not exist. It is a situation that no one yet dominates. A number of alternative routes to exploiting the opportunity and a number of different positions may remain viable indefinitely. When one superior path is identified, the situation evolves into an intersecting situation (6.4.5 Intersecting Situations).

5. In an open situation, each competitor is forced to choose among alternative routes. We must choose where we put our efforts and how much to invest in developing a position. Since we have limited resources, we cannot pursue all the possible alternatives involved. We must commit to one or the other of them (3.1.1 Resource Limitations).

Illustration:

Let us consider an open situation for the promotion to a new position at work. You are being considered for a job promotion. Others are also being considered. You still have time to prove yourself, but you don't know what the selection criteria will be. When you ask your boss directly what she is looking for, she tells you, "I don't know exactly, but I will know it when I see it."

1. A open situation occurs only in the middle of a campaign. The contest for the open job cannot exist without a group of potential candidates and some criteria, as yet unknown, for selection.

2. In an open situation, competitors have different options about how to pursue the opportunity. Candidates can emphasize a range of different types of skills and abilities in positioning for the job opening.

3. In an open situation, there is a race among competitors to discover the complete solution . A decision must be made in a limited amount of time. Only one candidate will best identify and best demonstrate a match for the job during that period of time. The contest is not the identification of the perfect person, but the best among the alternatives.

4. In an open situation, competitors are making different types of progress by using different methods. Candidates can have different strengths and weakness, but the relative value of those strengths and weakness in terms of filling the job are unclear and uncertain.

5. In an open situation, each competitor is forced to choose among alternative routes. Candidates must choose which of their various strengths to emphasize, which requires understanding the field of competitors, and a way of promoting those particular strengths as the most valuable for the job opening, which requires understanding the job and the decision-maker.

6.4.5 Intersecting Situations

Sun Tzu's five key methods for recognizing situations that bring people together.

"Everyone shares access to a given area.
The first one to arrive there can gather a larger group
than anyone else.
This is intersecting terrain."
                              Sun Tzu's The Art of War 11:1:21-23

"Thought is the organizing factor in man, intersected
between the causal primary instincts and the resulting
actions."
                                                  Albert Einstein

"One never reaches home, but wherever friendly paths
intersect the whole world looks like home for a time."
                                                  Hermann Hesse

General Principle: Intersecting situations force people to move on the same path.

Situation:

The challenge here is almost the opposite of that in the open situation. In the open situation, no one knows which path leads to a successful position. In the intersecting situation, everyone agrees on what a successful position is, but no one has the resources needed to create it. What we have discovered in the intersecting situation is that our path to success requires more resources than we have alone.

Opportunity:

All competitors vying for position have gathered enough information to see clearly what has to be done to successfully take advantage of an opportunity. Our opportunity here is that none of our rivals have the resources or skills needed to establish a successful position. This creates an opening within the opportunity, an opening within an opening (3.1.4 Openings).

Key Methods:

We recognize an intersecting situation by the following set of conditions.

1. An intersecting situation occurs only in the middle of a campaign. It is based on a more complete understanding of what is required to take advantage of an opportunity but the limited ability to execute based upon that understanding. In the beginning of a campaign, our understanding isn't complete enough to create an intersecting situation. The campaign ends when competitors are able to execute based on this understanding (6.3.2 Middle-Stage Situations).

2. In an intersecting situation, competitors share the same view of how to pursue the opportunity. Everyone agrees that there is only one path and set of methods that can be used to establish a position on the basis of the opportunity. Though everyone seeks to improve their own individual position, they realize that they share a mission in terms of the position that they want to establish (1.6.1 Shared Mission).

3. In an intersecting situation, no individual competitor has all the resources needed to establish a viable position. We all have limited resources. In this situation, each competitor's individual resources are not sufficient to establishing a position that can be successfully defended (3.1.1 Resource Limitations).

4. In an intersecting situation, competitors are tempted to join with others to create a complete solution and/or a dominant position. This is the natural result of seeing a shared mission. In this situation, no one yet dominates but everyone sees domination as possible. Sun Tzu describes this situation in terms of a "crowd under heaven," which I rendered rather clumsily as a "larger group than anyone else." This concept infers both completeness and relative superiority. 1.3.1 Competitive Comparison).

5. In an intersecting situation, there is a race among competitors to complete the solution. Those parties in the winning combination will succeed. The challenge is to be among the first competitors to establish a complete and productive position (5.3.1 Speed and Quickness).

Illustration:

As an illustration, let us use a common example that recurs frequently in high-tech. Several companies are bringing a new electronic device to market. The device requires complete integration among hardware, software, distribution, and service components. Hardware companies, software companies, device distributors, and service companies are all developing similar products for this market because they all see its potential. Each is ahead in their own area, but success will be determined by who will be able to create a complete product. Think about the recent, competition between Blu-Ray and HD-DVD as standards for the new generation of DVD player, a competition that Blu-Ray eventually won.

1. An intersecting situation occurs only in the middle of a campaign. The situation had to evolve to the point that there were competing technological camps promoting two different standards.

2. In an intersecting situation, competitors share the same view of how to pursue the opportunity. Everyone generally agrees about what the device requires in terms of capacity.

3. In an intersecting situation, no individual competitor has all the resources needed to establish a viable position. Sony (Blu-Ray) and Toshiba (HD-DVD) couldn't establish a standard on their own. They needed the support of other machine makers and those offering movie content.

4. In an intersecting situation, competitors are tempted to join with others to create a complete solution and/or a dominant position . Everyone saw the value of joining one camp or the other rather than having a divided market forever.

5. In an intersecting situation, there is a race among competitors to complete the solution. The question was, which one will get there first?

6.4.6 Serious Situations

Sun Tzu's six key methods for identifying situations where resources can be cut off.

"You can penetrate deeply into hostile territory.
Then many hostile cities are behind you.
This is dangerous terrain."
Sun Tzu's The Art of War 11:1:24-27

"The essential support and encouragement comes from within, arising out of the mad notion that your society needs to know what only you can tell it."
John Updike

"Support from a lack of new supply will be short-lived."
Makoto Yamashita

General Principle: Serious situations arise when distance and opposing forces makes it impossible to get more resources.

Situation:

The serious situation is not serious only in the sense of "grim" but also in the sense of "significant," as in a serious opportunity. In the serious situation, we have learned a great deal about the opportunity we are exploring. If the situation did not show the potential for more rewards, we would simply stop our move or campaign when our resources ran out. The fact that the situation evolves into a serious situation means the opportunity's potential has been, at least to some degree, verified.

Opportunity:

All competitors vying for position have gathered enough information to see clearly what has to be done to successfully take advantage of an opportunity. Our opportunity here is that none of our rivals have the resources or skills needed to establish a successful position. This creates an opening within the opportunity, an opening within an opening (3.1.4 Openings).

Key Methods:

There are six key methods for identifying serious situations.

1. A serious situation occurs when we are in the middle of a campaign after significant investments have been made in it. Time must pass to create a serious situation. The original resources we started with must have time to be exhausted. However, from that investment, we have learned enough about the potential reward to justify our desire to invest more (6.3.2 Middle-Stage Situations).

2. A serious situation requires distance between our position and the source of our resources. This distance is the central problem creating the serious situation. We encounter this situation when we are distant from our source of resources. We can only carry so many resources with us in making a move. Additional resources are needed from supporters over time. We are separated from those supporters because we have left them too far behind in our pursuit of an opportunity 4.4 Strategic Distance.

3. This distance can be either physical or intellectual. Physical resources require transportation over physical distances, but intellectual distance has perhaps a bigger affect our support. Our supporters require communication, which becomes more difficult as distance separates our perspective from theirs. Given our different perspectives, our supporters are less able to see the value of the campaign.(2.0 Developing Perspective).

4. The serious situation can only arise when we have verified some aspect of the opportunity's potential. In other words, we must know that the situation offers serious rewards and as well as a serious need for resources. If the nature of the opportunity didn't balance the additional costs, the move or campaign would simply end (8.0 Winning Rewards

5. A serious situation requires some lack of control over our supply lines. Distance alone raises the costs of transportation and communication, but it doesn't threaten it. The threat comes from our lack of control. If we had complete control of our supply lines, the serious situation could not develop. However, our control in this situation is limited due to some opposing force, whether a force of nature or conscious rival. This opposing force can cut-off our supply lines because of the distance involved (8.1.2 Reward Boundaries).

6. Serious situations often arise simply because campaigns continue longer than expected. This is often the case when our resources for a continued campaign rely on our supporters. Supporters naturally weary of campaigns and lose sight of the potential rewards. As campaigns continue, it often disappoints their expectations for a quick pay-off (8.1.3 Reward Timing).

Illustration:

The most famous historical example of the serious situation was Hannibal's campaign against Rome. Because Hannibal lost his support in Carthage, he eventually had to leave Italy without being defeated. Rome was given time to recover from the invasion, building up its army and eventually destroying Carthage entirely.

1. A serious situation occurs when we are in the middle of a campaign after significant investments have been made in it. This campaign took years, starting with the famous invasion over the Alps, but it continued up and down the Italian peninsula for years, through a series of battles.

2. A serious situation requires distance between our position and the source of our resources. Carthage was in northern Africa and Rome was in Italy. Hannibal required continued support from Carthage in order to continue the campaign.

3. This distance can be either physical or intellectual. The most important resource Hannibal needed was political. Over time, Hannibal's perspective grew more and more distant from that of the people in Carthage.

4. The serious situation can only arise when we have verified some aspect of the opportunity's potential. Hannibal saw both the wealth of Rome and the ease with which their armies were defeated. The Carthaginians saw only the continued costs of the campaign.

5. A serious situation requires some lack of control over our supply lines. Despite military success after military success against the Romans in Italy, Hannibal's political opponents in Carthage used Hannibal's absence to turn his supporters against him, cutting off any further support for his campaign.

6. Serious situations often arise simply because campaigns continue longer than expected. Hannibal's political opponents did not have a significant defeat to point to. Their problem was was simply the length and continued cost of the campaign.

6.4.7 Difficult Situations

Sun Tzu's six key methods for recognizing situations where serious barriers must be overcome.

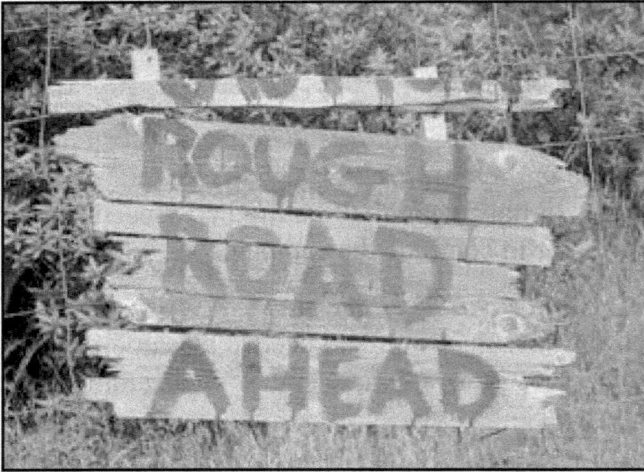

"There are mountain forests.
There are dangerous obstructions.
There are reservoirs.
Everyone confronts these obstacles on a campaign.
They make bad terrain."

Sun Tzu's The Art of War 11:1:27-31

Difficulties are things that show a person what they are.

Epictetus

"As we advance in life it becomes more and more
difficult, but in fighting the difficulties the inmost strength
of the heart is developed."

Vincent Van Gogh

General Principle: In difficult situations, progress slows down so much that we want to give up.

Situation:

The difficult situation is the something of the opposite of the Easy Situation (6.4.2 Easy Situations). Difficult situations arise when we encounter serious obstacles to success. They occur relatively late in a move or campaign, when we have completely explored an opportunity. The difficulties discovered can be a big problem central to the opportunity or a number of problems blocking all our different routes to success.

Opportunity:

In a difficult situation, we have the opportunity to establish a protected position (4.6.3 Barricaded Conditions). If the difficult situation doesn't stop us completely, we get through barriers that will hinder prospective competitors from following us.

Key Methods:

The following six methods help us clearly identify difficult situations.

1. *A difficult situation can occur only toward the end of a move or campaign.* Other situations can resemble a difficult situation because we encounter challenges or barriers, but the difficulty in a difficult situation is of a special kind. It is difficult both in the sense of representing significant barriers and also difficult in the sense that it causes us to worry about losing what we have invested in the move (6.3.3 Late-Stage Situations).

2. *In a difficult situation, we are committed because the move or campaign is close to a successful ending.* We are committed for two reasons. First, we know enough at this point to know that the opportunity has potential, which wins our commitment. Second, the more we invest in a move or campaign that has potential, the more committed we become to making it work. Though sunk costs should not influence our commitment to pursuing an opportunity,

those costs combined with the clearer view of potential creates commitment (6.2 Campaign Evaluation).

3. ***Difficult situations are challenging because progress slows to a crawl.*** A difficult situation arises from a dramatic slowdown in the pace of progress. Slower progress consumes resources, starting with our time, and discourages supporters. Supporters naturally weary of campaigns that are making little progress. They tend to lose sight of the potential rewards. As campaigns continue, it often disappoints people's expectations for a quick pay-off (8.1.3 Reward Timing).

4. ***Difficult situations are often created by earlier easy situations.*** Many campaigns that are easy at first naturally grow more difficult over time. The easy situation creates an expectation of continued quick progress. The subjective perception of slow progress is relative to our comparison with the earlier fast progress (6.4.2 Easy Situations).

5. ***In a difficult situation, the challenges engage us.*** If the problems were simply incomprehensible, the move would end, but in the serious situation, we appreciate the nature of the problem. Through the course of the move, we develop a deeper knowledge of an opportunity. As our distance from our initial position increases, we increase our knowledge of the new terrain. We learn more about the challenge of winning a position in it. The problem occupies our minds (4.4 Strategic Distance).

6. ***A difficult situation can arise when a variety of different obstacles block different potential paths.*** This usually happens when a difficult situation evolves from an open situation. In open situations, we can take a variety of paths to get to our goal. We and our different competitors can try a variety of paths. When we find these different paths blocked by different types of problems, the open situation changes into a difficult situation (6.4.3 Contentious Situations).

7. ***A difficult situation can arise from a single, large obstacle that was once hidden.*** This usually happens when a difficult situ-

ation evolves from an intersecting situation. In intersecting situations, everyone sees one, correct path to success. Since there is only one path to success, it can be blocked by a serious barrier, one that is perhaps impossible to overcome (6.4.5 Intersecting Situations).

Illustration:

As an illustration, let us consider a situation where you have been looking for a new job. You still have a job, but you think you see an opportunity to find a better one at another firm in the larger job market.

1. *A difficult situation can occur only toward the end of a move or campaign.* The situation is difficult because it has gone on for awhile and you are tiring of the process. The psychological effect of rejection is taking its toll. Your current job is looking better and better.

2. *In a difficult situation, we are committed because the move or campaign is close to a successful ending.* You have found that there are better jobs out there, but if something doesn't happen soon, you will give up the search. You have made it to the final interviews several times and have been told a number of times that you were the second choice, but you never get the job. You have been so close that you can taste it.

3. *Difficult situations are challenging because progress slows to a crawl.* You have already contacted all the likely prospects for employing you. It is becoming more and more difficult to find new prospects to contact.

4. *Difficult situations are often created by earlier easy situations.* You were initially surprised by how much demand there was for your skills set and job experience. When you sailed through to the final interview, you thought that the process would be much easier than it turned out to be.

5. *In a difficult situation, the challenges we discover truly engage us.* You find yourself thinking about the job hunt all the

time. You wonder why people don't want you. Even though you are still employed, the continuous rejections are eating at you.

6. *A difficult situation can arise when a variety of different obstacles block different potential paths.* In every situation, the problem seems to be different.

7. *A difficult situation can arise from a single, large obstacle that was once hidden.* You have the experience people are looking for, but the normal job qualifications for the position require more formal education than you have.

6.4.8 Limited Situations

Sun Tzu's six key methods for identifying situations defined by a bottleneck.

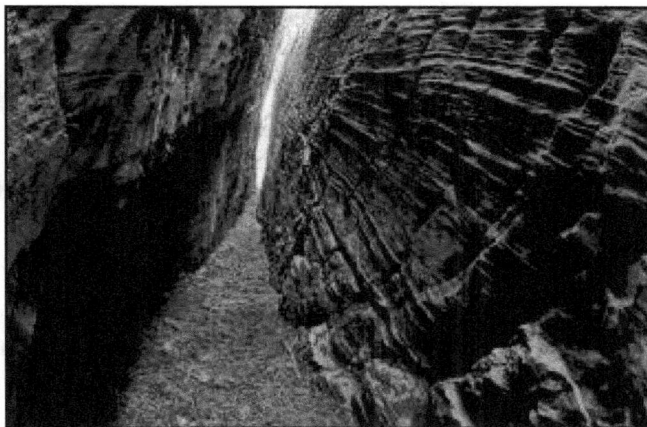

"In some areas, the entry passage is narrow. Y
ou are closed in as you try to get out of them.
In this type of area, a few people can effectively attack
your much larger force.
This is confined terrain."
Sun Tzu's The Art of War 11:1:32-35

The margin is narrow, but the responsibility is clear."
John F. Kennedy

"It keeps changing all the time, ... The narrow paths get
wider, the vistas open up as you walk through."
Ted Nierenberg

General Principle: In difficult situations, progress slows down so much that we want to give up.

Situation:

The Limited Situation marks a transition point when we depend on a narrow set of resources. In limited situations, we are constrained by our environment or surrounded by our opponents, making access to additional resources impossible. A limited situation occurs towards the end of a campaign where we are making the final transition to the desired position. This limited situation arises in an area where we cannot bring all our resources to bear because the transition point is a bottleneck.

Opportunity:

As in the difficult situation, a limited situation gives us the opportunity to establish a protected position (4.6.3 Barricaded Conditions). If we can get through the limited situation, we can, with very little work, create a barrier that will hinder prospective competitors from following us.

Key Methods:

The following six key methods are used to identify limited situations.

1. A limited situation can occur only toward the end of a move or campaign. A great deal of knowledge is required to get into a limited situation. We would not undertake the risks of a limited situation if we didn't know for certain that it was our only option and that the potential rewards of the opportunity were worth the risk. (6.3.3 Late-Stage Situations).

2. In a limited situation, the completion of a move is limited to a single path or a single type of resource. This is typically known as a "bottleneck." This bottleneck represents a transition point. The larger the total force making the transition, the more difficult the limited situation becomes(5.5.1 Force Size).

3. Competitive strength cannot exist at a limited situation's transition point. We create focused power by using **all** our available resources at once on a given move. In the limited situation, the nature of the situation prevents this. We can use only a fraction of our resources at a time of the transition point (5.5 Focused Power).

4. In a limited situation, we are vulnerable to relatively small challenges focused at the transition point. Bottlenecks limit production in a manufacturing environment but bottlenecks are vulnerabilities in a competitive environment. This is because opposition can oppose us at a transition point in the competitive environment. A challenge is any opposition to our move. Since we cannot bring all our resources to bear, even a relatively minor challenge can prevent our success (9.0 Understanding Vulnerability).

5. In a limited situation, our specific point of vulnerability is determined by the limited resource. There are five classical points of vulnerability. The nature of our vulnerability is determined by the people or the other materials that we need to complete the transition (9.1 Climate Vulnerability).

6. In a limited situation, the place and time of transition is known to us but not others. This transition point represents an opportunity window for our opponents, but as in all competitive situation, the information regarding that transition point is limited. If it was public, the point of transition would certainly be blocked and the situation would be either difficult or desperate (2.1.1 Information Limits]).

Illustration:

Let us illustrate this situation with an imaginary case study from the business world. A company has introduced a new product, but one of the components needed for that product is in short supply.

1. A limited situation can occur only toward the end of a move or campaign. The new product proves very popular on its introduction but because the supply of the needed component is limited, the manufacturer cannot ramp up production quickly enough, keeping the product from being a true success.

2. In a limited situation, the completion of a move is limited to a single path or a single type of resource. The component is currently available only from one small volume supplier. Others could make it but currently do not. There are no alternative components that will work in the current design.

3. Competitive strength cannot exist at a limited situation's transition point. The current supplier has little capability to expand, and, because of the component's limited supply, the product manufacturer has no leverage in negotiating with them.

4. In a limited situation, we are vulnerable to relatively small challenges focused at the transition point. If the product's popularity is discovered, many other companies can come out with competing products. Potential competitors will have enough time to do so if the original maker cannot get enough of their products onto the market to establish a standard and leadership.

5. In a limited situation, our specific point of vulnerability is determined by the limited resource. There are many components in the product, but only the one that is in limited supply matters. Both the component maker and potential competitors can use that vulnerability against the product maker.

6. In a limited situation, the place and time of transition is known to us but not others. At this point, neither the component manufacturer or competitors know about the product's potential popularity or the limited supply of the needed component.

6.4.9 Desperate Situations

Sun Tzu's three key methods for identifying situations where destruction is possible.

There is sometimes no place to run.
This is always deadly ground."
Sun Tzu's The Art of War 11:6:14-15

"When matters are desperate we must put on a desperate face."

Robert Burn

"Courage enlarges, cowardice diminishes resources.
In desperate straits the fears of the timid aggravate the dangers that imperil the brave."

Christian Nevell Bovee

General Principle: Desperate situations arise when everything is at risk.

Situation:

The Desperate Situation represents the class of situations where our position is deteriorating rapidly. A desperate situation occurs at the very end of a campaign when time, alternatives, and favorable conditions are all running out. Also known as the deadly or do-or-die situation, the desperate situation arises in an area where the forces opposing our success are rapidly mounting.

Opportunity:

The opportunity in a desperate situation is simple: to survive. Surviving a desperate situation is a form of "trial by ordeal," which proves the quality of the survivors. Surviving a desperate situation give us more credibility than the average person.

Key Methods:

The following three key methods allow us to recognize the desperate situation.

1. A desperate situation occurs only at the very end of a move when no other options are left. A desperate situation arises when we run out of other options. We would not get into a desperate situation if we had other alternatives (6.3.3 Late-Stage Situations).

2. In a desperate situation, conditions are deteriorating rapidly. We find ourselves in a desperate situation when conditions rapidly deteriorate. This negative shift in conditions may arise from environmental factors or from the actions of our rivals and opponents (1.3.1 Competitive Comparison

3. In a desperate situation, delaying our response is fatal. These conditions pose a threat to our existing established position as well as to the campaign. In the desperate situations, we must instantly recognize the threat and just as immediately respond appropriately (5.3 Reaction Time).

Illustration:

Let us illustrate the desperate situation with a health situation, one that actually happened to me personally.

1. A desperate situation occurs only at the very end of a move when no other options are left. You go to the doctor for what you think is a sinus infection. The doctor does some tests and discovers that you have cancer.

2. In a desperate situation, conditions are deteriorating rapidly. The cancer is in stage two, already spreading to other parts of your body.

3. In a desperate situation, delaying our response is fatal. If you do not pick the right treatment, you will die.

6.5.0 Nine Responses

Sun Tzu's twelve key methods for using the best responses to the nine common competitive situations.

"To be successful, you must control scattering terrain by avoiding battle. Control easy terrain by not stopping.
Control disputed terrain by not attacking.
Control open terrain by staying with the enemy's forces.
Control intersecting terrain by uniting with your allies.
Control dangerous terrain by plundering.
Control bad terrain by keeping on the move.
Control confined terrain by using surprise.
Control deadly terrain by fighting."

Sun Tzu's The Art of War 11:1:39-48

"A wise person does at once, what a fool does at last.
Both do the same thing; only at different times."

John Dalberg Acton

"He who hesitates is lost."

General Principle: Instantly know the right responses to meet the nine common situations.

Situation:

The nine classes of competitive situations develop naturally over the course of a move or campaign. While their development is natural, our successful resolution of these situations depends entirely on our choice of action. Our instinctual responses only lead us from one situation to the next, ending eventually at the desperate situation. This is the path we seek to avoid by training our responses. We can only successfully advance our position in these situations if we apply the right responses. The problem is that most of us simply do not understand those responses, at least not enough to use them instantly as a trained reflex.

Opportunity:

The faster we recognize and respond to these situations, the more certain our success becomes. Instantly recognizing these situations is the beginning of our training, but we must also know what response each common situation requires (6.4 Nine Situations). Reading about these responses is also just the beginning. We need to internalize the worldview required in order to develop instant strategic reflexes. You must respond to these situations automatically. We act best when we have correctly retrained our instincts.

Key Methods:

Let us start with the key methods of response and a simple list of the nine responses to the nine classes or situations.

1. We must use proven responses instead of doing what we feel like doing in the nine situations. Responding by how we feel simply leads us into more and more difficult situations. The appropriate responses have been proven over thousands of years of experience. These situations have occurred millions of times in competition and will recur again and again. We must be prepared to react appropriately when they arise by dealing with the situation pragmatically instead of emotionally (2.2.2 Mental Models).

2. We must respond appropriately to the nine situations instantly as a reflex. The longer we delay, the less likely our success becomes and the more likely it is that our current situation will evolve into another type of situation. The secret to our success is taking the right actions as a matter of reflex (6.1.1 Conditioned Reflexes).

3. The more creatively the nine responses are applied, the better they work. The responses themselves are specific, eliminating most other forms of action, but they allow for a wide variety of application. If we want to succeed consistently, we have to instantly know what each situation requires (7.0 Creating Momentum).

4. We respond to a dissipating situation by avoiding a meeting with the larger, attacking force. We cannot simply evade them because they are attacking our position, so we must defend by distracting them from the attack (6.5.1 Dissipating Response).

5. We respond to an easy situation by pressing forward with our advance. We avoid being easily satisfied with easy gains. Instead, we must be even more aggressive (6.5.2 Easy Response).

6. We respond to a contentious situation by avoiding challenging rivals for positions. We avoid getting drawn into direct confrontations (6.5.3 Contentious Response).

7. We respond to an open situation by keeping up with our competitors. We gauge our progress against theirs and copy whatever they do that is working (6.5.4 Open Response).

8. We respond to an intersecting situation by quickly forming partnerships. If we are the first to

9. form alliances, even with potential competitors, we can create the dominant position (6.5.5 Intersecting Response).

10. We respond to a serious situation by getting our resources from the opportunity. We make the new venture pay in any way that we can, even if only for the short term (6.5.6 Serious Response).

11. We respond to a difficult situation by continuing to move. No matter how slow and difficult our progress becomes, we cannot stop moving. We keep on, trying new angles for direction on the problem (6.5.7 Difficult Response).

12. We respond to a limited situation by keeping our move a surprise. Our actions during these transitions must be unexpected by being creative and unpredictable (6.5.5 Intersecting Response). **We respond to a desperate situation by committing everything.** We bring all our resources to bear as quickly as possible, holding nothing in reserve. (6.5.9 Desperate Response).

Illustration:

In the article on the nine situations (6.4 Nine Situations), we illustrated the classes of situations with a hairdresser opening a new salon. Let us extend that illustration here.

1. We must use proven responses instead of doing what we feel like doing in the nine situations. A hairdresser might want to just cut hair rather than respond to strategic conditions, but that simply doesn't work.

2. We must respond appropriately to the nine situations instantly as a reflex. No matter when one of these situations arises, the salon owner must deal with it immediately before it gets worse.

3. The more creatively the nine responses are applied, the better they work. Knowing the right response is a good beginning, but a creative response is much more powerful in terms of creating strategic momentum.

4. We respond to a dissipating situation by avoiding a meeting with the larger, attacking force. In this example, we played the role of hairdressers who started a salon because of a bad job market.

Starting a business works because it avoids expending resources on looking for jobs for which there is too much competition.

5. _We respond to an easy situation by pressing forward with our advance_. We started this business without a salon by visiting past customers in their homes to do their hair. Though we may find enough customers to make a decent income easily, we should continue to contact past customers, continuing to build the business.

6. _We respond to a contentious situation by avoiding challenging rivals for positions_. As our "athome" service attracts rivals, we should look for niches in the market that others have difficulty covering.

7. _We respond to an open situation by keeping up with our competitors_. If a rival finds a novel way of providing services that gives them an advantage, we should quickly copy it in our own niche.

8. _We respond to an intersecting situation by quickly forming partnerships._ As competition heats up, advertising becomes important, but the businesses in this market are too small to advertise. We should start an association of "home haircare providers" that can advertise and direct those interested to members of the association.

9. _We respond to a serious situation by getting our resources from the opportunity._ As a move takes more time, we have to get compensated for the time it takes. You start billing each member for a referral fee.

10. _We respond to a difficult situation by continuing to move_. In making the transition from a hairdresser to business owner to an association owner, we keep moving, slowly evolving our business role to fit evolving market needs.

11. _We respond to a limited situation by keeping our move a surprise_. We must make a decision, choosing between being a hairdresser and running the association. We choose to focus on the association but don't tell our hairdressing customers until the new business is established and stable.

12.   ***We respond to a desperate situation by committing*** ***everything.*** Some members start a competing association. We must respond quickly, devoting all our resources to bring them back into the original group because the market will not support two competing organizations.

6.5.1 Dissipating Response

Sun Tzu's five key methods for responding to dissipation by the use of offense as defense.

"To be successful, you must control scattering terrain by avoiding battle."

Sun Tzu's The Art of War 11:1:39

"Divide and rule, the politician cries; unite and lead, is watchword of the wise."

Johann Wolfgang von Goethe

"Words divide us, actions unite us."

Tupamoros Sloga

General Principle: In dissipating situations, we put our opponents on the defensive to rally our supporters.

Situation:

The Dissipating Situation arises when we are targeted for an attack by a capable foe and, as a result, our supporters are likely to desert us to protect themselves. The response must both protect an existing position while avoiding meeting an overpowering opponent. The critical danger of the dissipating situation is that it undermines the unity of our supporters (1.7.1 Team Unity).

Opportunity:

Our opportunity here starts with correctly identifying a dissipating situation, which helps us identify whether or not we can defend our position directly (6.4.1 Dissipating Situations). In a dissipating situation, our opportunity is to quickly change the priorities of our larger opponent by taking a quick and unexpected action. Therefore the real purpose of our response is to demonstrate leadership that unites our people by giving them a task to focus on (1.5.1 Command Leadership).

Key Methods:

These are the key methods for responding to a dissipating situation.

1. In a dissipating situation, we must identify unprotected resources that are valuable to our attacker. We discover what our attackers prize dearly. It can be their reputation, a relationship, a physical resource, or any other resources. This resource must have more proven value for them than the unproven value of fighting us for position. When someone focuses on attacking, they overlook what they must defend (1.1.2 Defending Positions).

2. In the dissipating situation, we advance toward the valued resource and away from the forces attacking us. In this situation, evading our attacking opponent is not enough. Since our position is threatened, we must advance toward something. Of course, a clever attack is better than a poor one, but the real issue is time: we must put together the best attack that we can launch immediately (6.1.1 Conditioned Reflexes).

3. *In a dissipating situation, we must make sure that our opponents know exactly what we are threatening.* While this move is not what our opponent expected, we don't make this advance in secret. The point here is not to win the targeted resource but to force our opponents to shift from an attack on our position to a defense of their own. Psychologically, people fear loss more than they value gain (loss aversion). This is the one situation where the best defense is a good offense (5.6.1 Defense Priority).

4. *In a dissipating situation, we seek to make attacking us more trouble than it is worth.* Whatever our attackers hoped to gain from attacking us is less important to them than losing something that they already have and value. By attacking what they prize, we are making ourselves more trouble than we are worth (1.6.3 Shifting Priorities).

5. *In a dissipating situation, going on the attack rallies our supports and unifies them.* If our supporters face an overwhelming threat, they will desert us, each giving a priority to their own personal defense. People naturally run away from danger. We harness this desire and, at the same time, provide them with a focus for their movement. People would rather move toward a goal than away from a threat. The job of the leader in this situation is to provide their supporters with a clear goal, increasing their strength and unity (1.7.2 Goal Focus).

Illustration:

In our article, on recognizing dissipating situations, we used the example of a large company threatening a smaller company's niche. Let us continue this illustration.

These are the key methods for responding to a dissipating situation.

1. In a dissipating situation, we must identify unprotected resources that are valuable to our attacker. We immediately identify what the invading organization is most proud of in their company's performance, standing, relationships, history, etc.

2. In the dissipating situation, we advance toward the valued resource and away from the forces attacking us. We then find a way to turn the attack against us into a direct threat to what they value. For example, if their organization publicly acclaims a value such as honesty, we find ways to demonstrate how the attack on our market is, above all, dishonest.

3. In a dissipating situation, we must make sure that our opponents know exactly what we are threatening. We make it clear that though they could probably win our market, we will use that battle to attack their reputation, fighting the battle in the media rather than in the market.

4. In a dissipating situation, we seek to make attacking us more trouble than it is worth. Their reputation for honesty must be more valuable to them than our niche of the market.

5. In a dissipating situation, going on the attack rallies our supports and unifies them. By making it clear how we are going to put the larger opponent on the defensive, we encourage our supporters,

6.5.2 Easy Response

Sun Tzu's five key methods regarding overcoming complacency.

"Control easy terrain by not stopping."
Sun Tzu's The Art of War 11:1:41

"Almost everything in life is easier to get into than out of."
Anonymous

"There's no thrill in easy sailing when the skies are clear and blue, there's no joy in merely doing things which any one can do. But there is some satisfaction that is mighty sweet to take, when you reach a destination that you thought you'd never make."
Spirella

General Principle: In easy situations, we make as much progress as quickly as we can.

Situation:

Of course, we must first know for certain that we are in an easy situation. If not, we can make a serious mistake in our response.

We describe the Easy Situation generally as when we first begin a move or campaign and make progress easier than we expect (6.4.2 Easy Situations). As a result, we form our expectations and attitudes about the future of our progress. These attitudes work against us as our move progresses. The danger is that these expectations lead us into patterns of behavior that set us up for failure.

Opportunity:

The easy situation is, by its nature, a tremendous opportunity if we can take it seriously. Of all the nine classes of situation, it offers us the most progress in advancing our position at the least cost. All we need to take advantage of this situation is to realize that it is a limited time offer (5.3.2 Opportunity Windows).

Key Methods:

When we start any campaign or project, we can never be surprised if our initial progress comes easily, and we must never let our initially easy progress change our behavior. The successful response to the easy situation requires us to instantly do the following:

1. In an easy situation, we must focus exclusively on making as much progress as quickly as we can. We keep going. We don't stop. We especially don't want to get distracted. This lesson goes back to Aesop's tale of *The Tortoise and the Hare*. The hare lost for one reason. He got so far ahead he felt that he could afford a break. The real danger of the easy situation is that it creates an expectation that we will not have to press hard to succeed. This lack of pressure leads to a lack of focus because it gives us time to get distracted (1.7.2 Goal Focus).

2. In an easy situation, we communicate our increasing control of the ground and concern about future problems. Our continued, *visible* progress creates the subjective impression that we own the position. Our expressions of concerns are taken more seriously because of our increased pressure. If we pause, we give others time to see an opportunity in what we have left undone. We want people to perceive our position as even more advanced than it is rather than have them doubt our enthusiasm. The subjective perception helps create the objective reality by changing the actions of others as well as our own (1.2 Subobjective Positions)

3. In an easy situation, we want to offer a moving target. Since we are making progress, others will be tempted to duplicate our efforts. They are more likely to be tempted into competition if they feel that they can catch up to us. This will allow them to make our lives difficult in any number of ways. (5.3.1 Speed and Quickness).

4. Until the easy situation ends, we press forward until we can reap rewards from our progress. Sun Tzu's strategy is not just about advancing our position but making our advances pay. We do not really control a position until our move pays for itself in tangible advantages. We want the easy situation to end with the reality of getting rewarded from our rapid progress (8.0 Winning Rewards)

5. Until the easy situation ends, we keep putting more resources into the move. Ideally, those resources come from winning rewards from the new opportunity, but this rule holds even if the position doesn't yet pay for itself. If we are not putting all our resources into an easy situation, where we are making the greatest progress, we are making a mistake. We want to put more resources into what is working so we are not tempted into putting more resources where we are not making progress. We will naturally find other outlets for our excess resources (3.3 Opportunity Resources).

Illustration:

We will continue the example we started in our discussion of identifying easy situations (6.4.2 Easy Situations). A group is given the task of designing a product for a specific market. The product development deadline is three months away at the beginning of the project. A group is given the task of designing a product for a specific market. After three weeks, they seem to have completed half of their project's goals.

These are the key methods for responding to a dissipating situation.

1. In an easy situation, we must focus exclusively on making as much progress as quickly as we can. In response to this easy progress, the team leader presses the team even harder toward completion.

2. In an easy situation, we communicate our increasing control of the ground and concern about future problems. The team leader communicates the team's fast progress to management but also voices concerns about the project hitting a future serious problem. The pressure on the team arises out of that concern.

3. In an easy situation, we want to present a moving target. In pressing forward, the team leader resists the pressure to expand the features being developed in the product.

4. Until the easy situation ends, we press forward until we can reap rewards from our progress. Instead of feature creep, the leader instead expands the scope of his project to include a market test, which will generate revenue.

5. Until the easy situation ends, we keep putting more resources into the move. The project leader seeks more resources, ideally from the market test, as a way of perfecting the design again based on feedback from the market test.

6.5.3 Contentious Response

Sun Tzu's five key methods for responding to contentious situations by knowing how to avoid conflict.

"Control disputed terrain by not attacking."
Sun Tzu's The Art of War 11:1:42

"The well-meaning contention that all ideas have equal merit seems to me little different from the disastrous contention that no ideas have any merit."
Carl Sagan

"Such democracies have ever been spectacles of turbulence and contention; have ever been found incompatible with personal security or the rights of property; and have in general been as short in their lives as they have been violent in their deaths."
James Madison

General Principle: In contentious situations, hamper your opponents, don't fight them.

Situation:

The contentious situation arises when we find that an opportunity is very rewarding, but, as a result, others are attracted to it as well (6.4.3 Contentious Situations). Contentious situations tempt us into conflict with others. If the opportunity being explored didn't offer potentially rich rewards, the risk of costly conflict would mean simply that it wasn't really worth pursuing (3.1.3 Conflict Cost). However, the potential for rich rewards changes not only our response, but what we can expect from others.

Opportunity:

Our primary goal is to further explore the situation while avoiding costly conflict. Since this is an early stage situation, we want to give the situation time to develop (6.3.1 Early-Stage Situations). If given the time, these situations often develop in open situations (6.4.4 Open Situations) or intersecting situations but only if we are able to avoid costly conflict (6.4.5 Intersecting Situations).

Key Methods:

In this specific situation, the following key methods govern our responses:

1. In contentious situations, we must respond instantly but against our basic impulses. We respond instantly to make fast progress because these situations naturally quickly degrade over time. Unfortunately, our two instinctual responses, the flight or fight reflex, both work against us in this situation as we explain below. Instead, we react instantly not on instinct but on the basis of training (6.1.1 Conditioned Reflexes).

2. In contentious situations, we cannot abandon the area of opportunity. The fact that the opportunity shows promise so early in the process, long before any positions are established, means we must focus on exploring it further, looking for a way to establish a position (5.2 Opportunity Exploration).

3. In contentious situations, we must go out of our way to avoid conflict with potential rivals. Conflict defines situations where a meeting is damaging to all participants. The easiest way to avoid conflict is to avoid such meetings on contentious ground (3.1.3 Conflict Cost).

4. In contentious situations, we seek to make ourselves less visible and threatening than opponents. We must not only avoid meeting potential opponents, but we must give them as little incentive as possible to come after us as a potential opponent. We need to keep a low profile in our exploration, attracting a minimum of attention (2.7 Information Secrecy).

5. In contentious situations, we hamper the progress of others in any way that we can. This rule is subordinate to the previous one. We must do this anonymously. We only do this in ways that cannot draw retaliation. With that in mind, we do not want to pass up any opportunities to slow our rivals down. One primary method is to use misdirection while working behind the scene (2.1.3 Strategic Deception).

Illustration:

The example that we discussed earlier in identifying a contentious situation was the early stages of a presidential campaign where a number of candidates are still in contention for their parties nomination (6.4.3 Contentious Situations). Let us continue with this illustration. In this case, let us assume we are the candidate.

1. In contentious situations, we must respond instantly but against our basic impulses. We must react quickly to the crowded field. In this case, we should have expected it.

2. In contentious situations, we cannot abandon the area of opportunity. We must not abandon the field simply because it is crowded.

3. In contentious situations, we must go out of our way to avoid conflict with potential rivals. During debates and other appearances, we must go out of our way not to attack any of our rivals. We can ignore them or even say nice things about them, but we must go out of our way not to damage them.

4. In contentious situations, we seek to make ourselves less visible and threatening than opponents. We should work as much as possible beneath the surface, raising money and putting together local organizations. Even in public forums, like debates, we should not attempt to be the star. If we shine before we have established our position, we will draw the fire of all the other candidates. We want to appear solid rather than threatening. It would be great if we could make all the other candidates think that we were actually running for the number two spot, with them as number one.

5. In contentious situations, we hamper the progress of others in any way that we can. Again, working behind the scenes, we should create challenges and problems for the other candidates when we can do it secretly. For example, if we find damaging information, we should not use it ourselves or even have our supporters use it. We should leak it to the press, or even better, to another rival.

6.5.4 Open Response

Sun Tzu's five key methods to help us keep up with the opposition.

"Control open terrain by staying with the enemy's forces."

Sun Tzu's The Art of War 11:1:42

"Plodding wins the race."

Aesop

"The trouble with the rat-race is that even if you win, you're still a rat."

Lily Tomlin

General Principle: In open situations, keep up with opponents.

Situation:

The Open Situation arises in the middle of a campaign when we are in a race with other competitors but the best route to success is not clear (6.4.3 Contentious Situations). Open situations challenge our ego on one hand and our herd mentality on the other. Ego is dangerous if the situation develops into a intersecting situation (6.4.5 Intersecting Situations). A herd mentality forgets the basic rule about opportunities being openings (3.1.4 Openings). These two attitudes can easily create a lagging position, which can degrade quickly in a serious situation (6.4.5 Intersecting Situations).

Opportunity:

Our primary goal in the open situation is not to get left behind (1.3.1 Competitive Comparison). As long as we can stay close to the race, our position is viable. Our opportunity is to remain within striking distance as these contests develop. Since this is a middle-stage situation, we must still explore the terrain. The end is not yet in sight (6.3.2 Middle-Stage Situations).

Key Methods:

We respond to the challenging realities of the open situation by following the following key methods:

1. In an open situation, we must quickly pick the route that seems best. Middle-stage situations are all different forms of a race. Speed is important in all strategic moves, but it is more important as we get into the middle stages of moves and campaigns and most important in the open situation where speed determines the winner (5.3.1 Speed and Quickness).

2. If several routes in an open situation seem equal, we must pick the path furthest from the others. This is the path in the the least popular area of exploration. If our route proves successful, we are actually in a better position because our path is less crowded and others will have more of a tendency to ignore us rather than their more proximate rivals (3.2.4 Emptiness and Fullness)

3. In an open situation, we keep in touch with what everyone else is doing. Responding to an open situation is like navigating a maze where we cannot know the right route. Chance plays a critical role in chaotic competitive environments. Anyone might stumble on the right route or many different routes may prove equal. When they do so, we need to know it as soon as possible. Though we hope our distance will help them ignore our progress, we cannot overlook theirs (1.8.4 Probabilistic Process).

4. If our progress in an open situation is equal to that of others, we must keep on the path that we have chosen. We must *not* switch our route even if the majority takes another route. If our progress along our alternative path is equal to that of others, we are better on our own path. This is not an intersecting situation where we get an advantage by joining with others (6.5.4 Open Response)

5. If others find an area in the open situation where progress is faster, we must instantly switch to that area. We must keep up with the leaders. We cannot stubbornly defend our path after we clearly fall behind others. This mistake is just another form of conforming to the pressure of our plans (5.2.1 Choosing Adaptability).

Illustration:

Let us continue the illustration that we started in discussing the identification of open situations (6.4.3 Contentious Situations). We are being considered for a job promotion. Others are also being considered. We still have time to prove ourselves, but we don't know what the selection criteria will be. When we ask our boss directly what she is looking for, she tells us, "I don't know exactly, but I will know it when I see it."

1. In an open situation, we must quickly pick the route that seems best. We must choose a course of action, say, increasing sales, that we think will impress our boss.

2. If we have several routes that seem equal, we must pick the route furthest from the others. If most of our rivals are working to develop one category of products, we pick another category of products that seems to have equal potential but as far away from them as possible.

3. In an open situation, we keep in touch with what everyone else is doing. We must track their progress and especially keep in contact with our boss to gauge how he feels about our progress relative to that of our rivals.

4. If our progress in an open situation is equal to that of others, we must keep on the path that we have chosen. We stick to our original choice of increasing the sales of a different category of products as long as our progress seems equal to the others in terms of making an impression on our boss.

5. If others find an area where progress is faster in an open situation we must instantly switch to that area. If another category of products becomes more important, especially in the mind of our boss, we immediately redirect our sales efforts. We publicly recognize our shift and how it is a response to the situation. We learn from our rivals' successful methods and try to improve on them.

6.5.5 Intersecting Response

Sun Tzu's five key methods on the formation of situational alliances.

"On intersecting terrain, you must solidify your alliances."

Sun Tzu's The Art of War 11:1:43

"Thought is the organizing factor in man, intersected between the causal primary instincts and the resulting actions."

Albert Einstein

"One never reaches home, but wherever friendly paths intersect the whole world looks like home for a time."

Hermann Hesse

General Principle: In intersecting situations, create the right alliances to quickly create a dominant situation.

Situation:

The Intersecting Situation arises when an opportunity takes all rivals to the same path, but none of those rivals have the size and strengths necessary to develop a winning position on it (6.4.5 Intersecting Situations). In this situation, being better than other competitors (1.3.1 Competitive Comparison) is not enough to be successful. The situation demands a particular set of skills and resources and it will take too long for anyone to develop those skills on their own (5.3.1 Speed and Quickness).

Opportunity:

Our opportunity in the intersecting situation is to put together the skills and resources needed to dominate the single path to success. Where no single competitor can dominate the situation, the first group of competitors to create a working alliance will always dominate the intersecting situation. The alliance only works if it is successful in establishing a new position and making that position pay (3.1 Strategic Economics). Intersecting situations leverage our herd mentality in a positive way.

Key Methods:

There are five key methods that define our response in an intersecting situation.

1. In an intersecting situation, we must start thinking about others in terms of shared goals. Since Sun Tzu's strategy is about improving position, rather than defeating enemies, the idea of an "enemy" is simply the idea of someone close to us with whom our position is compared. The fact that others are close to us in an intersecting situation creates the basis for a shared mission (1.6.1 Shared Mission).

2. In an intersecting situation, we look at the strengths *and weaknesses of our potential competitors in terms of potential fit.* Responding to the intersecting situation requires that we instantly form alliances with those with whom we might normally consider rivals or competitors. We must understand how our strengths and weakness fit with those of others around us (3.4.2 Opportunity Fit).

3. In an intersecting situation, we quickly join with others. The key here is speed. Since time is of the essence especially in middle-stage responses, we must make our choice of partners quickly. As in the school yard, those who pick first get the best choices (5.3 Reaction Time).

4. In an intersecting situation, we keep joining with others until we create a dominant position. A dominant position can be defined in terms of either the right combination of skills to make a complete product or simply by size. We want to create the type of force needed to clearly dominate the intersection (1.3.1 Competitive Comparison).

5. In an intersecting situation, we trade a smaller slice of the pie for more certainty. To make the alliance work, we must be willing to give up our personal preferences for the group goal. Within that larger mission, we can focus our own smaller area of control to create unity within the group (1.7 Competitive Power).

Illustration:

As an illustration, we used the common version of the intersecting situation that recurs over and over again in high-tech that we used when discussing how to recognize this situation (6.4.5 Intersecting Situations). Several companies are bringing a new electronic device to market. The device requires complete integration among hardware, software, distribution, and service components. Hardware companies, software companies, device distributors, and service companies are all developing similar products for this market because they all see its potential. Each is ahead in their own area, but success will be determined by who will be able to fill in the gaps in their offering to create the complete product. Think the recent, competition between Blu-Ray and HD-DVD as standards for the new generation of DVD player, a competition that Blu-Ray eventually won.

1. In an intersecting situation, we must start thinking about others in terms of shared goals. While everyone else is thinking how they can dominate this market, we start thinking about why some of these companies might want partners.

2. In an intersecting situation, we look at the strengths *and weaknesses of our potential competitors in terms of potential fit.* If we represent a software company, we are looking for hardware, distributors and service providers who would make good partners.

3. In an intersecting situation, we quickly join with others. We want to be the first company soliciting partners with whom to work.

4. In an intersecting situation, we keep joining with others until we create a dominant position. We make it clear that these are not exclusive partnerships, but that our association wants to help each member by creating a dominating market presence. Each member gets stronger by adding new members. The new members are not competitors. The real opponent is invisibility in the marketplace.

5. In an intersecting situation, we trade a smaller slice of the pie for more certainty. We want to keep dividing the pie to grow it until we push out any competing position in the market.

6.5.6 Serious Response

Sun Tzu's six key methods for responding to serious situations by finding immediate income.

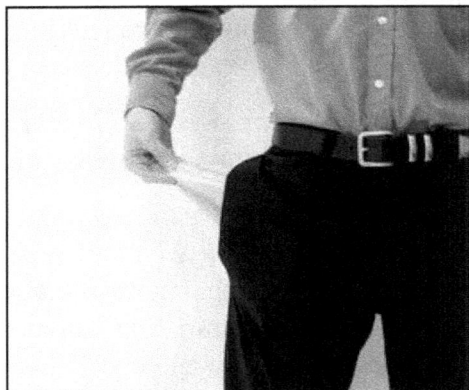

"Control dangerous terrain by plundering."
Sun Tzu's The Art of War 11:1:44

"The essential support and encouragement comes from within, arising out of the mad notion that your society needs to know what only you can tell it."
John Updike

"Support from a lack of new supply will be short-lived."
Makoto Yamashita

General Principle: In serious situations, refocus on finding local resources for survival.

Situation:

The Serious Situation arises when we lose our original source of support for a campaign or project. In a Serious Situation, we get further from our original sources of resources because we have gotten more deeply involved in the project. This positions us so that our support gets pinched off (6.4.6 Serious Situations).

Opportunity:

Our only opportunity in the serious situation is to work on resources generation (8.0 Winning Rewards1.8 Progress Cycle). While we c do only one thing at a time, we can switch our focus at any time to the claim step to get a partial award based on a partial move (8.2 Making Claims).

Key Methods:

In a serious situation, we must instantly move to get local resources in any way that we can. We respond to serious situations by:

1. As with all middle-stage situation, we must act quickly. Middle-stage situation are all different types of races. In this case, the race is to find more resources before our current supplies run out. The faster we adapt to our situation, the further ahead we will be (6.3.2 Middle-Stage Situations).

2. In a serious situation, we put our original targets on hold. If we are short on resources, we are no longer a serious competitor for the larger rewards of the opportunity. The first requirement for exploring an opportunity is the availability of resources (3.3 Opportunity Resources).

3. In a serious situation, we keep our shortage of resources a secret if possible. Resource shortage is a vulnerability. If others in our competitive arena know about our weakness, it will invite attack (2.7 Information Secrecy).

4. In a serious situation, we must identify any ways in which our current position can generate resources. This means looking for resources in the immediate vicinity, even if only for the short term. The resources must be strategically nearby because speed is critical here (4.4 Strategic Distance).

5. *In a serious situation, we must shift from longer-term exploration to short-term local exploitation.* A serious situation demands that we shift our internal mindset from the adventure of adaptive exploration to the boring nuts and bolts of scrabbling for resources. This requires a shift in mindset. Sun Tzu describes this as plundering or pillaging, but in modern competition, this isn't stealing resources from the local area as much as providing value to the local area in exchange for resources (1.2.2 Exploiting Exploration).

6. *In a serious situation, we must often get creative.* This is one of those situations where we must leverage adversity into creativity, doing something novel, new, and different (6.1.2 Prioritizing Conditions).

Illustration:

In our original explanation of how to recognize these situations, we used the most famous historical example of the serious situation, Hannibal's campaign against Rome. We will use this illustration to demonstrate both where he took the correct steps and why he failed to do so.

Hannibal's response to being cut-off from resources by Carthage was to rely more heavily upon his brother in Spain, develop alliances with local Italian tribes who were unhappy with Roman domination and with Philip V of Macedon. None of the sources provided enough resources to succeed in his campaign, especially after his brother, Margo, was defeated in Liguria and the breakdown of his alliance with Phillip. This returned him to Carthage in 203 BC.

In a serious situation, we must instantly move to get local resources in any way that we can. We respond to intersecting situations by:

1. *As with all middle-stage situations, we must act quickly.* Originally, Hannibal did act quickly to raise local resources which was why his campaign in Italy lasted for years. However, his biggest mistake was developing new channels of supply that were still too distant, in Spain and Greece.

2. *In a serious situation, we put our original targets on hold.* He failed here as. Psychologically, he was still dependent on support from Carthage. He did not secure his new channels of supply.

3. *In a serious situation, we keep our shortage of resources a secret.* This was difficult because his two main supply channels were too distant.

4. *In a serious situation, we must identify any ways in which our current position can generate resources.* Again, Hannibal was too dependent on his past position, as the leader of Carthage, rather than his new position and the occupier of Italy. He never really transitioned to a local ruler from an external conqueror.

5. *In a serious situation, we must shift from longer-term exploration to short-term local exploitation.* When he developed his local alliances, he should have worked more methodically at politically balancing his Italian allies against each other than relying on his own military control. He needed to use the politics of Italy in his favor rather than simply making alliances that could be easily betrayed, positioning himself as a necessary component in that balance. He should have promised the various city-states the extension of their local dominion at the expense of Rome while protecting them against each other. He had demonstrated his ability to defeat the Roman armies. He needed to position himself as the military champion of the local city-states. Instead, he presented himself as an alternative external ruler instead of simply a liberator and peace keeper.

6. *In a serious situation, we must often get creative* . The raw materials for victory were all there, but as a general rather than a politician, Hannibal couldn't put them together. He was unable to switch his competitive skills from the battlefield to the realm of politics.

6.5.7 Difficult Response

Five key methods regarding the role of persistence.

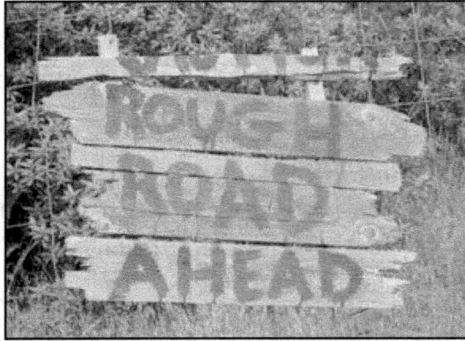

"Control bad terrain by keeping on the move."
Sun Tzu's The Art of War 11:1:45

"Winners never quit and quitters never win."
Vince Lombardi

"As we advance in life it becomes more and more difficult, but in fighting the difficulties the inmost strength of the heart is developed."
Vincent Van Gogh

General Principle: Overcome difficult situations through persistence and creativity.

Situation:

Difficult situations arise at the end of a campaign when we encounter obstacles that make progress much slower and more difficult than expected (6.4.7 Difficult Situations). While we are always interested in finding the path of least resistance to our goals, no path that takes us anywhere worth going is easy the entire way. The danger of the difficult situation is that it causes us to think that the grass must be greener somewhere else. Since beginnings are almost always easier than endings, it is always tempting to start a new project rather than finish an existing one (6.4.2 Easy Situations). People who skip from one thing to another without finishing anything are never successful.

Opportunity:

As we approach the successful end of a campaign, the clearest signs that we are succeeding is often mounting resistance and opposition (3.2.4 Emptiness and Fullness). The fact that we are getting more resistance is a symptom of the fact that we are getting close to success. Opponents redouble their efforts to stop us as we approach our goal. Our reaction to that opposition is the key. When we are not discouraged and press on, our persistence gives others the impression that our success is inevitable (1.2 Subobjective Positions).

Key Methods:

The following five key methods are key to winning a difficult situation.

1. We must keep our goal in sight during a difficult situation. A difficult situation is a late-stage situation where we have learned a great deal about the opportunity and its payoff. It is very different from a low-probability or any early-stage situation where the goal is distance and payoff uncertain. Lombardi's advice about "winners never quit," only applies to the difficult situation. It is a waste of resources if applied to situations where it is inappropriate (6.3.3 Late-Stage Situations).

2. In a difficult situation, we focus on making progress no matter how slowly. Notice the difference here between the late-stage difficult situation and a middle-stage situation where speed is a primary requirement for all responses. Speed is impossible in a difficult situation. Instead, we rely on focused power, taking one step at a time no matter how small (5.5 Focused Power).

3. In a difficult situation, we cannot turn back on the progress that we have made. A difficult situation is very different from an open situation where we are still choosing among various paths. This late in a campaign, the path is clear. We cannot abandon our progress to look for another path. We get rewarded faster by persisting through a difficult stretch at the end of a path than we do by abandoning that path (4.5.2 Surface Barriers).

4. In a difficult situation, we try different angles and invent creative ways to go forward. Sometimes we don't have to tackle the barrier directly. We can often find a faster, easier path, not by going back, but by trying different directions forward. Often we need to meet the challenge of a difficult situation in order to spark the creativity needed to create momentum. As with all late stage situations, innovation is especially important (7.3 Strategic Innovation).

5. In a difficult situation, we use our actions to eliminate doubts about our enthusiasm and commitment. The barriers in a difficult situation are both physical and psychological. We can often speed our progress by winning the support of others. When we persist, we create the perception that we are in control of the situation and win the support of others to help us through (9.3 Crisis Leadership).

Illustration:

In our illustration of how to correctly recognize this situation, we considered a situation where you have been looking for a new job. You still have a job, but you think you see an opportunity to find a better one at another firm in the larger job market (6.4.7 Difficult Situations).

1. We must keep our goal in sight during a difficult situation. In this example, you have discovered that people are looking for your talents and experience, but the standard job qualifications for the position require more formal education than you have. You must see the employer's need as more important than the obstacle, your lack of formal education.

2. In a difficult situation, we focus on making progress no matter how slowly. You persist in searching for the job you want by contacting more and more organizations. In making these new contacts, you bring up the problem, your lack of standard qualifications, at the beginning of the process to save time and to get decision-makers to eliminate the barrier early rather than using it as a tie-breaker later.

3. In a difficult situation, we cannot turn back on the progress that we have made. While you are making new contacts, this doesn't mean you forget about the companies where you were the second choice because of your formal training. You keep in touch with them in case their first choices do not work out.

4. In a difficult situation, we try different angles and invent creative ways to go forward. If you are creative, you can find a way to turn your more unique set of qualifications into a positive instead of a negative. If most of their people have those qualifications, your different success profile broadens their organization's spectrum of skills rather than duplicating the same skills that they already have.

5. In a difficult situation, we use our actions to eliminate doubts about our enthusiasm and commitment. While most organizations will stick to the formal standard, there will be a percentage who do not. That percentage will appreciate your persistence in facing the problem directly rather than trying to hide the problem or giving up when faced with it.

6.5.8 Limited Response

Sun Tzu's four key methods on the need for secret speed in tight situations.

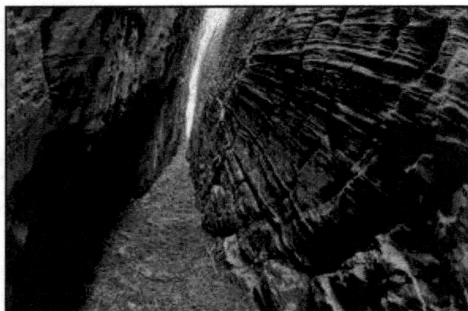

"Control confined terrain by using surprise."
Sun Tzu's The Art of War 11:1:46

"Whoever can surprise well must Conquer."
John Paul Jones

"It is surprising what a man can do when he has to, and how little most men will do when they don't have to."
Walter Linn

General Principle: In limited situations, we must secretly invent a surprise.

Situation:

The Limited Situation marks a transition point when we depend on a narrow set of resources. In limited situations, we are constrained by our environment or surrounded by our opponents, making access to additional resources impossible (6.4.8 Limited Situations).

Opportunity:

Our opportunity in a limited situation exists in our ability to use secrecy (2.7 Information Secrecy). Even if they suspect that our options or resources are limited, we can use that fact to set them up for a surprise, leveraging unpredictability against them (2.3.2 Reaction Unpredictability).

Key Methods:

A limited situation puts us in a highly vulnerable position in a late stage of our campaign. As we pass through the transition involved, we can be easily stopped. With this in mind, we respond to limited situations by:

1. In a limited situation, we keep our situation a secret. When we can only bring limited resources to defend or advance, our primary goal must be to keep others from recognizing our vulnerability (9.0 Understanding Vulnerability).

2. In a limited situation, we must give every appearance of being calm. When we are hemmed in and surrounded, we often give ourselves away because we panic. We don't want to be the rabbit that panics jumps up and exposes its hiding place at the approach of a coyote. If we remain calm in what appears to be a limited situation, our opponents must wonder what we know that they do not (2.1.1 Information Limits]).

3. In a limited situation, we use creativity to make the path of transition less predictable. All latestage responses require more creativity than other situations. In this situation, surprise is absolutely required. In limited situations, our actions seem predictable so we must use methods that are not predictable (7.0 Creating Momentum).

4. In a limited situation, we complete the transition out of our limited situation before others can block us. This is different from speed in the "race" situations of a campaign's middle-stages because we must finish our move before our opponents suspect it.

We must keep our hurry from attracting attention and triggering a reaction (5.3.1 Speed and Quickness).

Illustration:

We will extend the illustration we used in discussing how to identify these situations using an imaginary case study from the business world. A company has introduced a new product, but one of the components needed for that product is in short supply (6.4.8 Limited Situations).

1. In a limited situation, we keep our situation a secret. In purchasing negotiations with potential suppliers, the company should be discussing other, ideally much different, broader, and longer-term supply needs. These needs could be for totally fictitious future products, whose component demands are ideal for each vendor to whom they are talking.

2. In a limited situation, we must give every appearance of being calm. The company must not display any excitement about the success of their new product that requires the component in limited supply. The discussion of this component should only be brought up casually and tangentially, as a possible immediate test of suppliers' ability to deliver on the fictitious larger, longer term need.

3. In a limited situation, we use creativity to make the path of transition less predictable. By opening discussions with a number of different suppliers, we put pressure on existing suppliers who will hear about those discussions. We can discuss the needed component with the supplier who presently provides the required component based, not upon our desperate need, but upon their limitation in production, putting them on the defensive.

4. In a limited situation, we complete the transition out of our limited situation before others can block us. This approach will prevent suppliers from taking advantage of our immediate needs. The monopoly supplier cannot overcharge and competitors cannot use their existing relationships with potential alternative suppliers from undercutting the needed purchase.

6.5.9 Desperate Response

Sun Tzu's five key methods on when to use all our resources.

"Control deadly terrain by fighting."
                    Sun Tzu's The Art of War 11:1:47

"On deadly terrain, you must show what you can do by killing the enemy."
                    Sun Tzu's The Art of War 11:6:24

"Fight till the last gasp."
                    William Shakespeare

"It is surprising what a man can do when he has to, and how little most men will do when they don't have to."
                    Robert Louis Stevenson

General Principle: In desperate situations, we must use every resource we have.

Situation:

The Desperate Situation arises when our position is deteriorating rapidly and everything is at risk. The desperate situation is characterized by its lack of alternatives. We must make sure we identify our situation correctly, eliminating every other possible situation and response--which is why it is last in this series (6.4.9 Desperate Situations). The real risk of the desperate situation is that we delay making the difficult decision. The only alternative is that we simply give up, roll over, and die (6.8 Competitive Psychology). Unfortunately, more are killed running away from a losing battle, than fighting their way through it.

Opportunity:

This drastic response is an opportunity because it dramatically increases our chances of survival and success. The response required is so drastic that it can only be used in truly desperate situations. Since we have nothing to lose through conflict, but our opponents do, we can turn our weakness into a strength (3.5 Strength and Weakness) Our strength comes from knowing we are in a desperate situation before our opponents do so that our ferocity of response catches them unprepared and unwilling to take the risk of meeting us.

Key Methods:

The desperate situation is the exception that proves the general rule about avoiding conflict. In the desperate situation, everything is at risk. With this in mind, we respond to desperate situations by following the five key methods:

1. In a desperate situation, we instantly and directly engage the opponents who have trapped us. When we are in a desperate situation, our opponents grow in strength against us, making our demise inevitable. This is a situation where we want our opponents to clearly understand the threat we pose. We must not only fight with everything we have, but we must do so instantly and very visibly (5.3.1 Speed and Quickness).

2. In a desperate situation, we focus all our resources to the single point of engagement, holding nothing back. The goal here is to create a maximum of focused power in a minimum burst of time (5.5 Focused Power).

3. In a desperate situation, we seek to damage those who oppose us as much as possible. Our response must give opponents something to fear, something to lose. We make it clear that meeting us will be very expensive, hoping to raise the risks so that they are no longer worth the rewards. When we demonstrate our willingness to bring down our opponents with us, they have to reconsider their plans (3.1.3 Conflict Cost).

4. In a desperate situation, we seek to suprise our opponents with our ferocity. As with all latestage situation, surprise is always important. By surprising our opponents, we seize the initiative in the situation, forcing them to deal with our response. They not only have to reconsider their plans, but they must do so quickly, choosing their course in an instant because we leave them little time to do otherwise. People prefer avoiding loss over seizing gain so they will have a tendency to want to back down (7.4.2 Momentum Timing).

5. In a desperate situation, we must not press our luck. If our opponents blink and we get some breathing room, we must not press forward, hoping to turn a surprise into a big victory. We would not be in a desperate situation if a big victory was possible. In these situations, our definition of success means simply surviving so that we can evade defeat and find a more defensible position (3.1 Strategic Economics).

Illustration:

To use the same situation we did to illustrate how to recognize the desperate situation, a health challenge where you go to the doctor for what you think is a sinus infection. The doctor does some tests and discovers that you have cancer. This is a desperate situation that I personally survived.

1. In a desperate situation, we instantly and directly engage the opponents who have trapped us. You must instantly dedicate all your time and resources to fighting the cancer. You cannot avoid the problem. In my case, I quickly found out who the best doctors were, what the best treatment was regardless of monetary or other costs, and instantly committed to that course of treatment.

2. In a desperate situation, we focus all our resources to the single point of engagement, holding nothing back. You must be willing to sacrifice your comfort, your wealth, and accept long-term disability in order to survive.

3. In a desperate situation, we seek to damage those who oppose us as much as possible. You must not surrender your decisions to whatever doctor you happen to have, insurance companies, and, God forbid, the government bureaucracy. No one cares as much about your life as you do.

4. In a desperate situation, we seek to surprise our opponents with our ferocity. We must not be shy about questioning our doctor and expressing our willingness to make sacrifices. In my case, despite the pain associated with my radiation treatment, I challenged my doctors to do more, upping my radiation regardless of the pain.

5. In a desperate situation, we must not press our luck. When you get cleared of the cancer, you must avoid any activities that create more potential dangers. After getting cured of my cancer, I am much more careful about my health than I was before.

6.6.0 Campaign Pause

Sun Tzu's five key methods on knowing when to stop advancing a position.

"If you are too weak to fight, you must find more men. In this situation, you must not act aggressively.
You must unite your forces.
Prepare for the enemy.
Recruit men and stay where you are."

Sun Tzu's The Art of War 9:6:1-5

"The sword outwears its sheath, and the soul wears out the breast. And the heart must pause to breathe, and love itself have rest."

Lord Byron

General Principle: Know the key situations in which campaigns must be paused.

Situation:

While our movement to improve our position never stops, we must sometimes take a pause. We can only take what we have the strength to grasp. We get into trouble when we reach beyond our capabilities. When our resources are spread too thin, we become vulnerable. We reach barriers that we don't have the resources to overcome, we must regroup. The problem is that it is often difficult to recognize our situation. Mistakes in monitoring resources are easy while we are making progress. The faster we are going, the easier it is to forget to monitor our limited resources (3.1.1 Resource Limitations). The more we focus on fighting the battle, the easier it is to run low on ammunition.

Opportunity:

The opportunity when we reach our limits is to consolidate our gains. We must reset and focus on our internal situation rather than the external. This is our switch from winning new ground to better controlling it (1.2.2 Exploiting Exploration). It means making the mental transition from competitive positioning to production management (1.9 Competition and Production). and work on improving its organization. We leverage the natural force of a situation but within our always limited capacity.

Key Methods:

The following five key methods define different pausing situations and how we must deal with them.

1. When we grow low on resources, we build up our existing position rather than extend or advance it. The most important internal resources are: 1) temporary resources, 2) physical resources, 3) condition recognition, and 4) message communication. We must have excess resources to explore opportunities. We always want to advance our position, but if we use more resources than we have, we endanger our current position. While we pause, we organize our operations. We work to become more internally productive. We build up our resources (3.3 Opportunity Resources).

2. When the situation changes too quickly to get feedback, we pause and wait for change to slow. During chaotic conditions, a right decision can turn into a wrong decision in a second. Under these conditions, it is better to find a safe port and do nothing for awhile. These situations usually arise on fluid situations, where we described them earlier as "change storms" (4.3.2 Fluid Forms).

3. When the conditions around us require skills that we don't have, we pause to acquire those skills. Making great progress eventually takes us into unknown areas. We have to realize when we are getting out of our depth. When we don't understand what the situation requires, we cannot know where we are or see where we are going (1.5.2. Group Methods).

4. Pausing situations temporarily take priority over the other classes of strategic situations. When we reach these limits, either in our internal resources or the external environment, we must pause. In some situations, such as dissipating and desperate, the pause will be as short as possible. Fortunately, in these serious situations, external conditions affect our opponents as much as they do ourselves. There may be more to gain. It may be right in front of us, but we cannot reach out to take it without endangering our position (1.6.3 Shifting Priorities).

5. When we are in a pausing situation, we must not challenge our opponents. We must do as little as possible to attract the attention of our rivals. We must make the minimum adjustments necessary to keep up with our rival's movements and wait until we have excess resources again and see the path to pursue clearly (1.3.1 Competitive Comparison).

Illustration:

A common illustration that we use for explaining strategic movement is navigating traffic. To reach our goal, we still have to deal on a case-by-case with the traffic we encounter on the path.

1. When we grow low on resources, we build up our existing position rather than extend or advance it. In this analogy, this principle says simply that we must not forget to check our gas tank during the trip. Even if it looked like plenty when we started out, it can run low if we get stuck in traffic.

2. When the situation changes too quickly to get feedback, we pause and wait for change to slow. If we have to make a turn, we have to wait for an opening in the traffic to do so.

3. When the conditions around us require skills that we don't have, we pause to acquire those skills. We cannot use the high-capacity lanes unless we stop and pick up a passenger.

4. Pausing situations temporarily take priority over the other classes of strategic situations. We have to deal with other standard situations in traffic, such as traffic jams, but we have to deal with these pausing conditions first.

5. When we are in a pausing situation, we must not challenge our opponents. We shouldn't push it to see how far we can get without running out of gas or force on-coming traffic to brake in order to make a turn.

6.7.0 Tailoring to Conditions

Seven key methods regarding overcoming opposition using conditions in the environment.

"Some military commanders do not know how to adjust their methods. They can find an advantageous position. Still, they cannot use their men effectively."
Sun Tzu's The Art of War 8:1:19-21

"The one who adapts his policy to the times prospers, and likewise that the one whose policy clashes with the demands of the times does not."
Niccolo Machiavelli

General Principle: Certain specific conditions determine how we adapt to overcome opposition.

Situation:

Movement often naturally generates opposition. Many of the nine common classes of strategic situations are defined by our position relative to opposition (6.4 Nine Situations). These same types of situations arise over and over again but they are never exactly the same. Every occurrence involves a unique constellation of conditions. As with all aspects of situation response, the devil is in the details.

Opportunity:

To minimize the impact of opposition, we have the opportunity to leverage the most specific conditions in our general situation. In addition to knowing the basic response a given situation requires, we can also know how to leverage certain conditions to our advantages (6.5 Nine Responses). Remember, our goal is never simply beating the opposition. Our goal is improving our position. In facing opposition, we must get past it to get to our goal. We must do this as easily and quickly as possible to accomplish our mission.

Key Methods:

The following seven key methods defined the major types of conditions to which we must adjust.

1. Dominant conditions are primarily determined by the physical form of a competitive arena. There are four primary forms: tilted, fluid, soft, and ideal. Three forces determine the key conditions of these forms of ground: gravity, currents, and solidity. (6.7.1 Form Adjustments).

2. Gravity is the most important condition on tilted forms of ground. These are areas where the force of gravity favors one relative direction is over another. We always want the gravity on our side (4.3.1 Tilted Forms).

3. Current direction is the most important condition on fluid forms of ground. These are areas where the force of change favors one direction over another. We want to move with the current and not against it (4.3.2 Fluid Forms).

4. Solidity is the most important condition on soft or uncertain forms of ground. Some locations and situations are much more solid and dependable than most locations around them. Here, we want the sparse support that is available, such as solid information, on our side (4.3.1 Tilted Forms).

5. Relative size and strength are the most important conditions on ideal forms of ground. Ideal forms are those in which the forces of gravity, currents, and solidity do not create a clear advantage. On this ground, it is the nature of the meeting forces, not our location on the ground, that determines our success (4.3.4 Neutral Form).

6. Relative size is the most important condition at the moment of meeting. This relative comparison is used to choose the exact best behavior to minimize the cost of dealing with opposition. Both large and small forces have certain advantages and disadvantages. How we respond when we have an overwhelming force is different than how we respond when we have a merely dominant force. Even if we are overwhelmed or dominated in size of force, we can turn the situation around by using the weaknesses of size (6.7.2 Size Adjustments).

7. Relative strength is the most important condition over the course of the contest. Strength conditions arise from the relative breadth, depth, and clarity of competing philosophies, goals, or missions. Strength comes from the uniting and focusing power of a mission. Different types of mission have different types of power. In each of these areas defining strength, the issue is not just recognizing what conditions are but in knowing how which advantages are on our side (6.7.2 Size Adjustments).

Illustration:

Let us illustrate these ideas using examples from product marketing.

1. Dominant conditions are primarily determined by the physical form of a competitive arena. When we are running a business, we tailor our responses to adjust to the conditions of our marketplace, that is, the customers and potential customers to whom we sell.

2. Gravity is the most important condition on tilted forms of ground. When a marketplace is dominated by a few large customers, positions supported by one of those customers is much more important than a position supported by a lot of the small ones.

3. Current direction is the most important condition on fluid forms of ground. In fast-changing marketplaces such as high-tech, we must not position ourselves against the dominant trends in the standards of the industry. If our customers are currently adopting certain standards, we must lead the trend and not follow it.

4. Solidity is the most important condition on soft forms of ground. In marketplaces that are very fickle and uncertain, such as the marketplace that is constantly changing where no one really knows what the trend is, we use a rare verifiable fact to support our marketing. For example, in the book market, most new book sales are uncertain and most fail. The only solid areas are popular authors, such as Sun Tzu, who sell year after year.

5. Relative size and strength are the most important conditions on ideal forms of ground. These are marketplaces with lots of similar customers. In these markets, one year's sales are very much like the previous year's. Change in them follows predictable cycles.

6. Relative size is the most important condition at the moment of meeting. In ideal markets, when the products of two competitor's meet in the marketplace, the companies selling those products must choose their distribution methods depending on their relative size. Large companies can try to be everywhere, surrounding the competition. Small companies must look for small niches evading the competition.

7. Relative strength is the most important condition over the course of the contest. After the initial meeting, the success of our marketing depends on: 1) focusing on customers' needs and 2) developing relationships with customers.

6.7.1 Form Adjustments

Sun Tzu's four key methods on adapting our responses based on the form of the ground.

"To win your battles, never attack uphill."
Sun Tzu's The Art of War 9:1:4

"Never face against the current."
Sun Tzu's The Art of War 9:1:13

"You must keep on the water grasses. Keep your back to a clump of trees.
This is how you position your army in a marsh."
Sun Tzu's The Art of War 9:1:18-20

"The gravity is the first thing which you don't think."
Albert Einstein

"Time is a sort of river of passing events, and strong is its current; no sooner is a thing brought to sight than it is swept by and another takes its place, and this too will be swept away."

Marcus Aurelius

"Although our intellect always longs for clarity and certainty, our nature often finds uncertainty fascinating."

Karl von Clausewitz

General Principle: When meeting opposition, know how to leverage the character of the ground.

Situation:

As we are moving to a new position, we meet opposition. To make our responses more effective, we want to leverage the the physical, persistent conditions of our environment, known as the "ground" (1.3.2 Element Scalability). Where we meet that opposition, that is, the type of ground that we are on, is critical to making the best decisions about how to respond. Different forms of ground offer us different types of advantages. We cannot leverage the different forms of ground unless we understand where its force lies.

Opportunity:

When we meet opposition, we can be on three forms of ground: a) highly uneven ground, b) fast changing ground, or c) very uncertain ground (4.3 Leveraging Form).

Key Methods:

The following four key methods describe how we use the form of the ground to improve our responses.

1. The force of the ground arises from the form of the ground.
There are three valuable ground forces: gravity, currents, and solidity. They become important on tilted, fluid, and soft forms of

ground, respectively. On these three forms of ground, their related forces give an advantage to one location over another (4.3 Leveraging Form).

2. *On tilted ground, we get the gravity on our side.* Inequality defines tilted forms. On tilted ground, the physical or psychological conditions favor certain locations over others. We get these forces on our side or get on the side of these forces (4.3.1 Tilted Forms).

3. *On fluid ground, we must move with the current of change.* This means avoiding the dominant, stable fixtures in the environment and siding with the changing ones. Dynamics define fluid forms. On fluid ground, the physical or psychological force of change favors a flow that avoids stable points (4.3.2 Fluid Forms).

4. *On soft ground, we must get the islands of stability on our side.* This means avoiding areas where the direction of change is uncertain. Uncertainty defines soft forms. On soft ground, the force favors physical or psychological points of stability. The key to using this ground is to identify those rare, stable features in the environment and using them. (4.3.1 Tilted Forms).

Illustration:

Let us use a variety of different examples to illustrate the different forms of grounds and how we tailor our responses.

1. *The force of the ground arises from the form of the ground.* Business and political situations arise on different ground. While business always depends on customers and politics always depends on voters, customers and voters are very different based on their geographical and demographic area. Knowing these differences allows us to work with the right forces.

2. *On tilted ground, we get the gravity on our side.* Inequality defines tilted forms. One form of uneven ground is a market dominated by a few large customers. If challenged by a rival in such a market, find the positions supported by these dominant customers that your rival has opposed. Use those positions to stand (keep existing customer) and move (win new customers) against these rivals.

3. On fluid ground, we must move with the current of change. One form of fluid ground is the personal technology hardware market, where the coming thing always dominates the established thing. If challenged by a rival in such a market, leverage the coming thing against their support of the established thing; netbooks over notebooks (see this article on Acer's rise over Dell) or a Pre, Droid, or Nexus One over iPhone.

4. On soft ground, we must get the islands of stability on our side. One form of soft ground is today's financial markets. Given the uncertain financial future--depression or recovery, inflation versus deflation, etc--we must focus our investments on what little that we know for certain: Government spending and US deficit is going through the roof.

6.7.2 Size Adjustments

Sun Tzu's seven key methods regarding adapting responses based on the relative size of opposing forces.

"The rules for making war are:
If you outnumber enemy forces ten to one, surround them.
If you outnumber them five to one, attack them.
If you outnumber them two to one, divide them.
If you are equal, then find an advantageous battle.
If you are fewer, defend against them.
If you are much weaker, evade them."

Sun Tzu's The Art of War 3:3:12-18

"Though your enemy is the size of an ant, regard him as an elephant."

Danish Proverb

General Principle: When meeting opposition, the relative size of force suggests the appropriate response.

Situation:

The problem is that the size of force, that is, the number of our supporters, can be a complicated topic. The relative size of forces are easily miscalculated because we know our resources much better than those of others (2.1.1 Information Limits). The result is that we overestimate what we can do. The result is costly conflict where even the "winner" can lose.

Opportunity:

The appropriate use of force is dictated by economics of strategy (3.1 Strategic Economics). Our first goal is to minimize the mistakes in using force that create conflict (3.1.3 Conflict Cost). Size has both value and costs. These costs include the dis-economies of scale.

Key Methods:

There are seven key methods describing the correct methods of dealing with the relative balance of forces.

1. Both we and our opponents are likely to overestimate the relative size of our supporting forces. We should assume both mistakes in our calculations. These mistakes will result in misjudgments. All the other principles are designed to avoid making mistakes based on this fundamental error (2.1.1 Information Limits]).

2. Rather than attacking with overwhelming force (10 to 1), we simply surround our opponents. We hem them in so that they must confront the futility of their situation. Our goal is to get them to surrender without a fight (2.6 Knowledge Leverage).

3. Using dominant force (5 to 1), we go directly after our opponents leaving them a clear outlet for retreat. This size advantage is so large that opponents are not likely to want to stand and battle.

Our goal is to win our position with a minimum of costly conflict (3.1.3 Conflict Cost).

4. Using larger forces (2 to 1), we divide our opposition. This advantage is small enough that either we or our opponents might miscalculate the situation. We therefore seek to handle smaller groups of opponents one at a time. Our larger force is not in itself sufficient to chase a relatively smaller opponent from the field (5.4 Minimizing Action).

5. Using equal forces (1 to 1), we avoid meeting the opponent until we can find the right situation. With equal forces, we must seek to leverage the ground against our opponents. We need to lure our opponents into ground positions where they are at a serious disadvantage (6.7.1 Form Adjustments).

6. Using a smaller force, we only meet opponents in defense of a well-fortified position. Defending always requires fewer resources than attacking. We concentrate our forces in a highly defensible position, resisting the opponent's attempt to draw us out (1.1.2 Defending Positions).

7. Using a much smaller force, we evade the opposition. We use our relative advantage in speed against their relative advantage of size. We strike where they are unprepared and fall back before they can mount a response (3.4 Dis-Economies of Scalee-alone link]).

Illustration:

Let us illustrate these key methods with a battle of office politics where we are opposing a policy that a rival is attempting to introduce.

1. Both we and our opponents are likely to overestimate the relative size of our force. We and our rival within an office probably both think that we have more support in the office than we really have.

2. Rather than attacking with overwhelming force (10 to 1), we simply surround our opponents*. If virtually everyone is on our side, we set up an "intervention" where we force our rival to confront our universal opposition.

3. Using dominant force (5 to 1), we go directly after our opponents leaving them a clear outlet for retreat*. We are going to have a showdown but, before we do, we make sure of two things. We must make sure that they can see how large our support is and give them a way to save face and back down.

4. Using larger forces (2 to 1), we divide our opposition*. Since our opponent has a significant number of supporters, we keep them from getting together. We stage separate meetings consisting of all of our supporters with a few of our opponent's supporters.

5. Using equal forces (1 to 1), we avoid meeting the opponent until we can find the right situation*. We could set up a meeting on tilted ground. We set up our showdown with a big boss in the meeting, who we know supports our point of view. The supporter of our opponent will be afraid to voice their support.

6. Using a smaller force, we only meet opponents in defense of a well-fortified position*. We do not get into any open battle with our opponent. Instead, we keep to areas of responsibility where we clearly have that authority to decide and our opponent does not.

7. Using a much smaller force, we evade the opposition*. We do not engage in direct opposition. Instead, we fight a guerrilla action, opposing the policy behind the scenes. We work secretly to disrupt the decision.

6.7.3 Strength Adjustments

Sun Tzu's nine key methods on how to adapt responses based on relative strength of opposing missions.

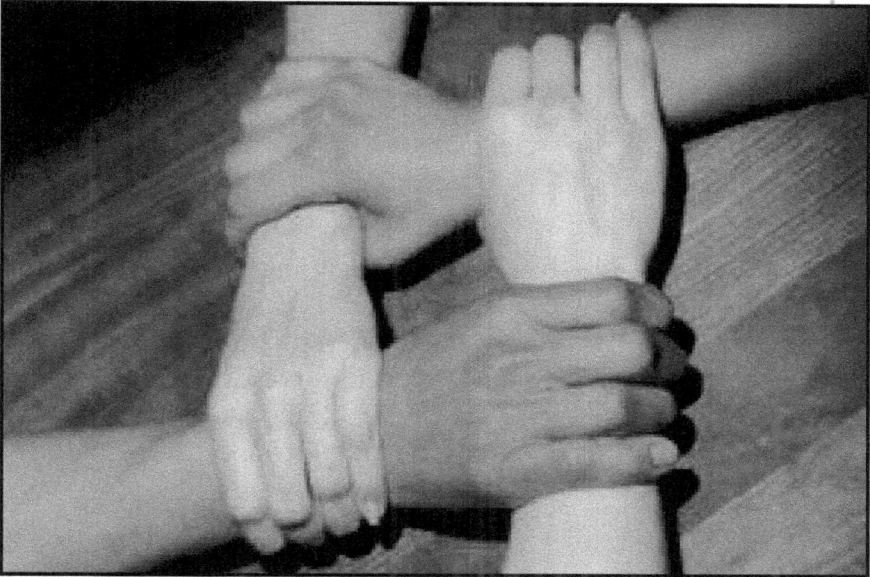

"You must control your field position. It will always strengthen your army."

Sun Tzu's The Art of War 10:3:1-2

"Only one who devotes himself to a cause with his whole strength and soul can be a true master. For this reason mastery demands all of a person."

Albert Einstein

"We confide in our strength, without boasting of it; we respect that of others, without fearing it."

Thomas Jefferson

General Principle: When meeting opposition, the relative strength of opposing missions tells us the best response.

Situation:

When we meet opposition, we also have to consider our relative strength versus our opponent's. Strength comes internally from our mission and externally from how well our mission fits a given position. Position strength is a very different strategic concept from size of forces, but it relates directly to our shared dedication to a mission.

Opportunity:

Our opportunity is to use our internal strength to create external strength. We can compare the internal strength of organizations in three different dimensions: 1) dedication to mission (1.6 Mission Values and 1.7 Competitive Power), 2) unity (1.7.1 Team Unity), and 3) focus (1.7.2 Goal Focus). External strength arises in the fit between these dimensions of mission and the opportunity dimension of a given position (4.6 Six Benchmarks).

Key Methods:

There are nine key methods describing how we adjust to conditions of relative strength.

1. Broad missions provide the strength needed for broad positions. Area breadth describes how inclusive or exclusive a position, an opportunity, or a mission are. A broad mission is generally a low level mission that most people share, for example, the desire for economic gain. A narrow mission is one that appeals to a smaller, more specialized group of people. The extremes of area are *spreadout* and *constricted* positions (4.5.1 Surface Area).

2. Deep missions provide strength to surmount high barriers. Deep missions are required to overcome serious barriers. Depth of mission describes how heavily committed people are to a particular mission. The level of commitment can be either deep or shallow. Often, the greater the breadth of a mission, the shallower its depth.

High-level missions both require and instill in people a deeper commitment. The two extremes of barriers are the barricaded position and the wide-open position (4.5.2 Surface Barriers).

3. Clear missions provide strength for positions that require holding power. Clarity describes the ease with which a mission, an opportunity, or a position are understood. Mission clarity describes how concise, transparent, and believable a set of goals are. Clear goals have an advantage when we want to increase a position's holding power. Clear goals have an advantage in depth, but fuzzy goals have an advantage in breadth. The extremes of holding power are *fixed* positions--extremely sticky-and *loose* positions--extremely loose (4.5.3 Surface Holding Power).

4. Spread-out positions must be supported by larger groups of people, which require a broader mission. Broad missions appeal to larger groups of people. Spread-out positions cannot be held by narrow groups, no matter how deep their commitment. In spread-out positions, we must broaden our mission to attract allies (4.6.1 Spread-Out Conditions).

5. Constricted positions can be defended by relatively small groups with narrow missions. These positions can survive on narrow missions appealing to smaller groups. Broad groups cannot access constricted positions. Confined positions cannot be accessed by broad groups. In confined positions, we must narrow our mission to our elite core (4.6.2 Constricted Conditions).

6. Wide-open positions are more easily captured by shallow missions. These positions are more popular, but they are always difficult to defend. In wide-open positions, we must emphasize the most shallow aspect of our mission to generate support that is easy to hold (4.6.3 Barricaded Conditions).

7. Barricaded positions require a depth of dedication to capture and are always easily defended. In barricaded positions, we must narrow our mission to its most dedicated core (4.6.4 Wide-Open Conditions).

8. *Fixed positions are more easily captured and defended by clear missions.* Clear missions are easier to understand and remember. These characteristics are part of the holding power of a fixed position. In fixed positions, we must clarify and simplify our mission so people understand and remember it (4.6.3 Barricaded Conditions).

9. *Loose positions are better suited to fuzzy missions.* These positions have little holding power so we have to be prepared to move on from them. Fuzzy positions can be more easily adapted to changing circumstances. In loose positions, we must keep our mission flexible so we can adapt it when we are forced to move (4.6.6 Sensitive Conditions).

Illustration:

All of these key methods are easily illustrated by the types of positions taken by politicians.

1. *Broad missions provide the strength needed for broad positions.* A politician running for national office must have a broader mission and take broader positions than one running for local office. "Make the world safe for Democracy" during WWI.

2. *Deep missions provide strength to surmount high barrier s.* A politician hoping to make serious changes to well-established policies must have deeper support than one who is willing to go with the flow. "All men are created equal" in the Civil war.

3. *Clear mission provides strength for positions that require holding power.* If a politician takes a clear stand on an issue, he will get deeper support, but it is much harder for him to change that position later. "Read my lips, no new taxes" was very clear.

4. *Spread-out positions must be supported by larger groups of people, which require a broader mission.* The broadest missions are economic. "It's the economy, stupid!" works in almost every age.

5. Constricted positions can be defended by relatively small groups with narrow missions. Legalization of marijuana is easier to establish in a city than in a state or the nation.

6. Wide-open positions are more easily captured by shallow missions. National campaigns are usually conducted on the basis of a very general mission such as "Hope" and "Change."

7. Barricaded positions require a depth of dedication to capture and are always easily defended. There were many historical obstacles to eliminating slavery or expanding voting to women, but, once it was abolished, defending the new position was easy.

8. Fixed positions are more easily captured and defended by clear missions. Conservative politicians defend well-established economic and social norms with missions that make clear distinctions between right and wrong.

9. Loose positions are better suited to fuzzy missions. Progressive politicians prefer vague positions because they seek to change society and the results are often hard to define other than in general terms such as "fairness" and "social justice."

6.8.0 Competitive Psychology

Sun Tzu's nine key methods for improving competitive psychology even in adversity and failure.

"You must control your soldiers with esprit de corps. You must bring them together by winning victories. You must get them to believe in you."
Sun Tzu's The Art of War 9:7;7-9

"What counts is not necessarily the size of the dog in the fight; it's the size of the fight in the dog."
Dwight David Eisenhower

General Principle: Responding quickly and appropriately to situations creates a psychological advantage.

Situation:

Responses that are inappropriate to our situation fail no matter how completely we are committed to them. However, half-hearted and uncertain responses can fail even if they are technically correct. Psychology is a critical component to all success. Making a serious commitment to a response focuses our efforts. Lack of commitment dissipates our efforts. If we are decisive in making the wrong decisions, we are simply reckless and undermine people's respect in us.

Opportunity:

Our ability to respond quickly and appropriately to challenging situations creates confidence in our supporters and fear in our rivals. To lead people, we must welcome challenges. Challenges give us the opportunity to demonstrate our ability to others. We must always make our supporters feel like they are winners. We do this by knowing what the psychology of the situation requires. If we show others that we can respond to both good and bad turns of events, they will support us. People will have no choice but to give us their respect. This is how we win the commitment of supporters and deference of opponents.

Key Methods:

At each stage of a campaign, we have to understand the psychology of creating supporters instead of opponents. No matter how difficult a situation gets, if we know what we are doing, we can use those difficulties themselves to bring people together rather than abandon us. The following nine key methods describe the psychological goals of each of the nine classes of common situations.

1. To succeed in the dissipating situation, we need to win the commitment of our supporters. The response to this situation is designed to unite people by giving them a mission (6.5.1 Dissipating Response).

2. In an easy situation, we use rapid progress to excite our supporters. We keep that progress going because making progress together unites people (6.5.2 Easy Response).

3. In a contentious situation, we pit our rivals against each other. We support everyone in their battles against every one else (6.5.3 Contentious Response).

4. In an open situation, we win supporters by pioneering a unique path. We win supporters away from rivals who are competing along similar paths (6.5.4 Open Response).

5. In an intersecting situation, we must get others to join us as partners. We do this by creating a shared mission to which everyone can contribute (6.5.5 Intersecting Response).

6. In the serious situation, we find ways to immediately create value for which others will reward us. Our psychological focus must shift to the needs of others (6.5.6 Serious Response).

7. In the difficult situation, we must give our supporters confidence. As our progress slows down, we must assure them that slow but sure wins the race (6.5.7 Difficult Response).

8. In the limited situation, we make a show of confidence while we focus on secrecy. We make sure that our competitors do not know that we are vulnerable (6.5.5 Intersecting Response).

9. In a desperate situation, we must focus our supporters on taking action. We prove ourselves by succeeding in the face of crisis (6.5.9 Desperate Response).

Illustration:

In the article on the nine situations (6.4 Nine Situations), we illustrated the nine classes of situations with a hairdresser opening a "hair cuts at home" business. We continued that example in the article on responses (6.5 Nine Responses). Let us finish that illustration here.

1. To succeed in the dissipating situation, we need to win the commitment of our supporters. We must directly ask our customers to support our business, getting them to commit to at least try our service. Once they do, they are less likely to waiver.

2. In an easy situation, we use rapid progress to excite our supporters. We must involve our customers in our success. We must communicate with them as our new business moves forward. We must thank them for their contribution, giving them ownership in our success.

3. In a contentious situation, we pit our rivals against each other. As others copy our methods, we should welcome them and offer to advise and help them against their competitors, that is, each other. We make them feel friendly toward us while hostile toward others.

4. In an open situation, we win supporters by pioneering a unique path. We must emphasize to our customers how our business is taking a different path than our new competitors. We make them feel special for choosing us.

5. In an intersecting situation, we must get others to join us as partners. We build on the friendships we have formed to create our advertising association. By asking them to join us, we acknowledge their worth and what we have in common.

6. In the serious situation, we find ways to immediately create value for which others will reward us. We create fear among members of our association that they will fail if the association cannot support itself.

7. In the difficult situation, we must give our supporters confidence. Though progress is slower, we praise everyone for their persistence, assuring them that it cannot help but be successful.

8. In the limited situation, we make a show of confidence while we focus on secrecy. Though we are making a secret transition, we are careful not to "go silent," making people suspicious.

9. In the desperate situation, we must focus our supporters on taking action. We must elevate the mission to an almost spiritual level as we ask for our supporters for their last full measure of commitment.

6.8.1 Adversity and Creativity

Sun Tzu's nine key methods for how we can use competitive challenges to spark our creativity.

ADVERSITY
Impossible odds makes achievements even more satisfying.

"To command and get the most out of proud people, you must study adversity."
Sun Tzu's The Art of War 12:4:12

"Necessity is the mother of invention, it is true, but its father is creativity, and knowledge is the midwife."
Jonathan Schattke

"Adversity reveals genius, prosperity conceals it."
Horace

General Principle: Facing competitive difficulties pressures us into increasing our capacity for creativity.

Situation:

There is a seeming paradox at the heart of Sun Tzu's strategy. His system teaches us to seek easy victories, avoiding difficulties, but he also teaches that only by facing difficulty can we reach our true potential. If an advance goes easily, we don't need to be inventive. If we minimize our mistakes, our efforts fail painlessly (5.0 Minimizing Mistakes). That failure leaves us somewhat wiser, but it doesn't thrust greatness upon us. Fortunately, this paradox goes away when we realize that difficulties, no matter how hard we try to avoid them, always find us.

Opportunity:

Our opportunities come from openings but those openings exist because of the unavoidable difficulties of life. As we make progress, our challenges inevitably become more difficult. It is only a matter of time until our advance becomes so difficult that we need to make a real breakthrough. This section of The Playbook deals with responding to situations (6.0 Situation Response). The next section deals with the role of creativity in Sun Tzu's strategy (7.0 Creating Momentum).

Key Methods:

In a campaign, we face a succession of challenges (6.3 Campaign Patterns). As these situations become more challenging, the role of creativity becomes more critical, as the following nine key methods demonstrate.

1. In dissipating situations, we learn what our attacker values and create a way to threaten it. We invent a response that exposes their weaknesses to our speed over their size(6.5.1 Dissipating Response).

2. In easy situations, we learn to control our expectations and create as much progress as possible. We invent a response that prevents us from relaxing (6.5.2 Easy Response).

3. In contentious situations, we learn how to avoid conflict and create obstacles for others. We invent a response that prevents others from relaxing (6.5.3 Contentious Response).

4. In open situations, we learn where our opponents are and create our own unique path. We invent a response that separates us from others (6.5.4 Open Response).

5. In the intersecting situation, we learn the skills and goals of others and create partnerships. We invent a response that brings us together with others (6.5.5 Intersecting Response).

6. In the serious situation, we learn about local resources and create a way to harvest them. We invent a response that brings us more local resources (6.5.6 Serious Response).

7. In the difficult situation, we learn the nature of the obstacles and create a path through them. We invent a response that moves us slowly forward (6.5.7 Difficult Response).

8. In the limited situation, we learn our limitations and create a surprise based on them. We invent a response that moves us secretly forward (6.5.5 Intersecting Response).

9. In the desperate situation, we learn to let go and create chaos. We invent a response that uses all our resources to threaten damage to opponents (6.5.9 Desperate Response).

Illustration:

Below are some inventions that came out of each of these different classes of situations.

1. In dissipating situations, we learn what our attacker values and create a way to threaten it. Google Apps were designed to threaten Microsoft's desktop dominance when Microsoft went after Google's search business.

2. In easy situations, we learn to control our expectations and create as much progress as possible. Apple's progress with the iPod, leading to the iTunes and the App Store are great examples of not resting on your laurels.

3. *In contentious situations, we learn how to avoid conflict and create obstacles for others*. The creation of various new technological standards are often designed to give one group an advantage over another.

4. *In open situations, we learn where our opponents are and create our own unique path*. In building their airplane, the Wright brothers kept track of developments in Europe but based their approach primarily on their background in bicycle making.

5. *In the intersecting situation, we learn the skills and goals of others and create partnerships*. William Durrant in starting General Motors brought together a number of small car companies to compete with Ford.

6. *In the serious situation, we learn about local resources and create a way to harvest them*. After years of growing famous for inventing great ideas that other companies capitalized on, XEROX finally made its PARC laboratory an independent company in 2002, forcing it to pay its own way, selling not only to XEROX but other companies as well.

7. *In the difficult situation, we learn the nature of the obstacles and create a path through them*. Years of failure in Iraq finally lead to the "surge" strategy, which brought an end to the war there and which now seems to be working in Afghanistan.

8. *In the limited situation, we learn our limitations and create a surprise based on them*. The transition of IBM from a mainframe computer company to a computer service company after the biggest financial loss in history was done so smoothly that most people never even realized that it was taking place.

9. *In the desperate situation, we learn to let go and create chaos*. The Tet Offensive by North Vietnam was a huge military disaster, but it was just as huge a PR bonanza, creating history's first successful in "media war," turning the US media against the success of their country on the battlefield.

6.8.2 Strength in Adversity

Sun Tzu's seven key methods on using adversity to increase a group's unity and focus.

"Use adversity correctly.
Tether your horses and bury your wagon's wheels.
Still, you can't depend on this alone.
An organized force is braver than lone individuals.
This is the art of organization.
Put the tough and weak together."
                                    Sun Tzu's The Art of War 12:4:15-20

"In prosperity, our friends know us; in adversity, we know our friends."
                                    John Churton Collins

"Sweet are the uses of adversity."
                                    William Shakespeare

General Principle: The shared threat of adversity can draw people together creating the unity that is the basis of group strength
.

Situation:

The pressure of opposition, as William Shakespeare observed, can be used by wise leaders. One of its uses is to bond people together in the face of a shared threat. Under dire circumstances, people naturally cling to the relative safety of groups. However, when put under certain kinds of pressure, groups can also fall apart (6.4.1 Dissipating Situations). To understand how adversity can create strength or weakness in a group, we have to understand the underlying principles by which Sun Tzu's strategy defines strength.

Opportunity:

That fear of loss is greater even than the desire for gain. Since adversity threatens individuals with loss, they naturally join with others who share their problems, challenges, and risks. Revolutions and political movements are born of adversity, not prosperity.

Key Methods:

The following seven key methods describe how adversity creates strength within organization when leaders know how to respond.

1. The strength of a group under adversity comes from shared goals. This sense of mutual danger and risk during times of adversity binds the group together. (1.7 Competitive Power).

2. Adversity can be used to close the gaps between self-interest and group interest that cause division. Weakness results from any influence that causes a group's members to put their own personal interests above those of the group. We use outside pressure, a common enemy, to draw people together (6.4.1 Dissipating Situations).

3. Adversity makes it more dangerous for members to leave the group. We must make it so their personal situation is more dangerous if they do. No form of motivation is stronger than our desire to protect ourselves. People feel more protected in a group (2.1.2 Leveraging Uncertainty).

4. Under pressure, we organize group members so that they have to rely on each others' strengths. Sun Tzu describes this as putting the weak with the strong and the experienced with the inexperienced (3.5 Strength and Weakness).

5. During times of stress, we control information so everyone gets the same message at the same time. Gaps between self-interest and group interest arise naturally when people are working from different information. The more people share information, the stronger the group becomes (2.2 Information Gathering).

6. We use adversity to move members closer together physically and psychologically. Again, weakness comes from the space between people. Separation in mind and body leads to division in goals (4.4 Strategic Distance).

7. Properly communicated, adversity gives more meaning to people's actions within the group. Everyone can have their own individual goals, but it is the commander's job to connect all the individual contributions to the whole. This is easier when there are common dangers and everyone can see each others contribution clearly (1.6.3 Shifting Priorities).

Illustration:

Let us apply these key methods to a business during a time of economic recession.

1. The strength of a group under adversity comes from shared goals. If people within the business understand that their job security depends on their business's profitability rather than the general economy, they will be stronger in a recession.

2. *Adversity can be used to close the gaps between self-interest and group interest that cause division*. If some employees see that they are making valuable contributions while others are just coasting, they will realize that the weak employees are threatening them personally, not just the company's profits.

3. *Adversity makes it more dangerous for members to leave the group*. During a recession, not even the more marketable members of the firm want to look for another position. Instead, they can be focused on making the company more successful.

4. *Under pressure, we organize group members so that they have to rely on each others' strengths*. We want to make the employees themselves responsible for each others' productivity. If they each understand that they must create value to justify their jobs, they will help each other do that and help identify the weak links that cannot contribute.

5. *During times of stress, we control information so everyone gets the same message at the same time*. We should make incomes and expenses more visible to everyone so everyone can understand where their paycheck is coming from. People should understand that companies don't print their own money, but that they can only survive from customer sales. If the sales aren't there, then expenses must be cut somewhere, eventually threatening them.

6. *We use adversity to move members closer together physically and psychologically*. We can use this as an opportunity to close separate offices or outlying businesses, moving people into less space focusing on fewer products, so people work more closely physically and mentally.

7. *Properly communicated, adversity gives more meaning to people's actions within the group*. Everyone should be challenged to relate their contribution to increasing sales, decreasing costs, and retaining customers.

6.8.3 Individual Toughness

Sun Tzu's eight key methods on how failure develops character.

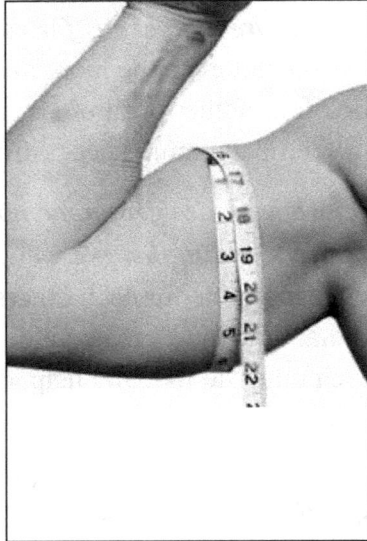

"You can be weakened in a deadly battle and yet be stronger afterward."

Sun Tzu's The Art of War 12:4:15-20

"All the adversity I've had in my life, all my troubles and obstacles, have strengthened me...You may not realize it when it happens, but a kick in the teeth may be the best thing in the world for you."

Walt Disney

"We acquire the strength we have overcome."

Ralph Waldo Emerson

General Principle: Only by facing adversity do we develop the individual strength of confidence.

Situation:

We must explore the borderlands between what is safe and what is foolhardy to be successful. The end result of opening ourselves to the world of possibilities is eventually meeting adversity. No matter how good our training in strategy, our encounters with adversity cannot always result in progress. If failure becomes a habit, we learn little from it. Those who drift wherever life takes them never learn from adversity and failure. Only a dead fish floats downstream.

Opportunity:

We can learn from our failures, but only if we have the right perspective and take action. Sun Tzu's principles work to make failure the exception rather than the rule by building position. Adversity and failure offer valuable resources that we can get nowhere else. We develop resilience and toughness only by meeting adversity and failure. Those for whom everything comes easily are poorly prepared for serious campaigns, which usually grow progressively more difficult over time (6.3.3 Late-Stage Situations).

Key Methods:

There are eight key methods for developing personal toughness from adversity and failure.

1. To develop personal toughness, we must expect the unexpected. The world is not under anyone's control. Life is not only unfair, but it is unpredictable and uncertain (2.3.2 Reaction Unpredictability).

2. To develop personal toughness, we must see success over time as likely. Sun Tzu's principles are all based on probabilities, not certainties, but they are essentially optimistic. They view progress as increasingly certain if we work to improve our position in reasonable ways. The world is not a deterministic machine. The world is an array of complex stochastic processes. We rely on high-probabilities over the long-term but know that many setbacks must occur over the short term (1.8.4 Probabilistic Process).

3. To develop personal toughness, we seek to minimize our maximum loss and maximize our minimum gain. We must expect failures and only seek to minimize them (5.0 Minimizing Mistakes).

4. To develop personal toughness, we restrain ourselves during a crisis. Overreacting to difficulties only makes them worse (4.2 Choosing Non-Action).

5. To develop personal toughness, we must prepare for situations to reverse themselves. This is true both for good and bad situations when they are outside of our control. As conditions reach their extremes, the more likely they are to reverse (3.2.4 Emptiness and Fullness).

6. To develop personal toughness, we must preserve our resources for future challenges. We avoid going "all in" except in the most desperate situations. We regularly accept little failures so that we always survive to fight another day (5.6.1 Defense Priority).

7. To develop personal toughness, we use repeated practice to lose our fear of failure. Fear is the mind killer. While we never accept failure, we can learn to take it in stride. We can do this only through exercises that retrain our normal emotional reactions (6.8 Competitive Psychology).

8. To develop personal toughness, we develop the courage to try again differently. Courage is a critical ingredient to decision-making. It describes our ability to accept uncertainty and take reasonable risks in pursuing our goals (1.5.1 Command Leadership).

Illustration:

Let us illustrate these key methods with how their reverse is being promoted today through the media. Much of this media message arises out of the messenger's desire to promote a certain form of politics.

1. To develop personal toughness, we must expect the unexpected. When a hurricane like Katrina strikes, the message is that such events should always be predictable and even controlled. Nothing is further from the truth.

2. To develop personal toughness, we must see success over time as likely. If we watch the news, we *know* the world is getting worse. But the reality is that by any objective analysis, as John Stossel's demonstrated in a recent show on "Life is Getting Better." The "man-bites-dog" bad news stories get reported while the "dog-bite-man" stories of every day success do not, giving everyone an upside-down view of life.

3. To develop personal toughness, we seek to minimize our maximum loss and maximize our minimum gain. What gets promoted in the media are the big gambles that pay-off, making life seem a matter of simple luck. This viewpoint is fueled by Hollywood, where the most successful realize that luck plays a major part in their success and therefore think that it must be a large component in everyone else's success as well. The truth is that there are very few areas, show business being one of them, where chance plays such a major role.

4. To develop personal toughness, we restrain ourselves during a crisis. During a crisis, the media always promotes the idea that the government must take action and then more action. Any idea of limited resources, priorities, and restraints are pushed out the window. The media never reports on the costs in lives and fortune that such extremes of action actually entail. When the debt bomb explodes from taking unnecessary actions, we will all pay for it.

5. To develop personal toughness, we must prepare for situations to reverse themselves. Human society is resilient and people adjust to change as a group without being directed to do so. In science, we say that complex, adaptive systems are inherently stable because we learn. The net effect is Sun Tzu's view of a world created of balancing complementary opposites. In such a world, crisis tend to right themselves at a minimum of costs as long as government or the media does not force individuals to make choices that they would not otherwise make on their own.

6. *To develop personal toughness, we must preserve our resources for future challenges.* We must save resources so we have extra resources to deal with the inevitable reversals of fortune. The idea that government or insurance companies can protect us from anything ever going wrong discourages such saving. This creates what is known as "a moral hazard," where we are willing to take risks that others must pay for.

7. *To develop personal toughness, we use repeated practice to lose our fear of failure.* The media encourages our fear and helplessness in the face of forces too large for us to control. Instead of acting and practicing decision-making, we are encouraged to become arm-chair critics, critiquing the imperfect judgments of others with 20/20 hindsight. By going through decision exercises, such as those we use in our Warrior Class Training, we learn that perfect judgment is not possible in every situation and that judgment can only become better when we are allowed to fail.

8. T*o develop personal toughness, we develop the courage to try again differently.* The media doesn't celebrate the idea that people should be and are personally rewarded for their courage. Indeed, courage is only portrayed in the media as a selfless act. What this actually encourages is fear and uncertainty because no one can understand the personal benefits of courage over time.

Glossary of Key Concepts from
Sun Tzu's *The Art of War*

This glossary is keyed to the most common English words used in the translation of *The Art of War*. Those terms only capture the strategic concepts generally. Though translated as English nouns, verbs, adverbs, or adjectives, the Chinese characters on which they are based are totally conceptual, not parts of speech. For example, the character for conflict is translated as the noun "conflict," as the verb "fight," and as the adjective "disputed." Ancient written Chinese was a conceptual language, not a spoken one. More like mathematical terms, these concepts are primarily defined by the strict structure of their relationships with other concepts. The Chinese names shown in parentheses with the characters are primarily based on Pinyin, but we occasionally use Cantonese terms to make each term unique.

Advance (*Jeun* 進): to move into new **ground**; to expand your **position**; to move forward in a campaign; the opposite of **flee**.

Advantage, *benefit* (*Li* 利): an opportunity arising from having a better **position** relative to an **enemy**; an opening left by an **enemy**; a **strength** that matches against an **enemy's weakness**; where fullness meets emptiness; a desirable characteristic of a strategic **position**.

Aim, *vision, foresee* (*Jian* 見): **focus** on a specific **advantage**, opening, or opportunity; predicting movements of an **enemy**; a skill of a **leader** in observing **climate**.

Analysis, *plan* (*Gai* 計): a comparison of relative **position**; the examination of the five factors that define a strategic **position**; a combination of **knowledge** and **vision**; the ability to see through **deception**.

Army: see **war.**

Attack, *invade* (*Gong* 攻): a movement to new **ground**; advancing a strategic **position**; action against an **enemy** in the sense of moving into his **ground**; opposite of **defend**; does not necessarily mean **conflict.**

Bad, *ruined* (*Pi* 圮): a condition of the **ground** that makes **advance** difficult; destroyed; terrain that is broken and difficult to traverse; one of the nine situations or types of terrain.

Barricaded: see **obstacles.**

Battle (*Zhan* 戰): to challenge; to engage an **enemy;** generically, to meet a challenge; to choose a confrontation with an **enemy** at a specific time and place; to focus all your resources on a task; to establish superiority in a **position**; to challenge an **enemy** to increase **chaos**; that which is **controlled** by **surprise**; one of the four forms of **attack;** the response to a **desperate situation;** character meaning was originally "big meeting," though later took on the meaning "big weapon"; not necessarily conflict.

Bravery, *courage* (_Yong_ 勇): the ability to face difficult choices; the character quality that deals with the changes of **CLIMATE;** courage of conviction; willingness to act on vision; one of the six characteristics of a leader.

Break, *broken, divided* (_Po_ 破): to divide what is **complete**; the absence of a **uniting philosophy**; the opposite of <u>unity</u>.

Calculate, *count* (_Shu_ 數): mathematical comparison of quantities and qualities; a measurement of **distance** or troop size.

Change, *transform* (_Bian_ 變): transition from one **condition** to another; the ability to adapt to different situations; a natural characteristic of **climate**.

Chaos, *disorder* (_Juan_ 亂): **conditions** that cannot be **foreseen**; the natural state of confusion arising from **battle**; one of six weaknesses of an organization; the opposite of **control**.

Claim, *position, form* (_Xing_ 形): to use the **ground**; a shape or specific condition of **ground**; the **ground** that you **control**; to use the benefits of the **ground**; the formations of troops; one of the four key skills in making progress.

Climate, *heaven* (_Tian_ 天): the passage of time; the realm of uncontrollable **change**; divine providence; the weather; trends that **change** over time; generally, the future; what one must **aim** at in the future; one of five key factors in **analysis;** the opposite of **ground**.

Command (_Ling_ 令): to order or the act of ordering subordinates; the decisions of a **leader**; the creation of **methods**.

Competition: see <u>war.</u>

Complete: see <u>unity.</u>

Condition: see **ground.**

Confined, *surround* (_Wei_ 圍): to encircle; a **situation** or **stage** in which your options are limited; the proper tactic for dealing with an **enemy** that is ten times smaller; to seal off a smaller **enemy**; the characteristic of a **stage** in which a larger **force** can be attacked by a smaller one; one of nine **situations** or **stages**.

Conflict, *fight* (_Zheng_ 爭): to contend; to dispute; direct confrontation of arms with an **enemy**; highly desirable **ground** that creates disputes; one of nine types of **ground,** terrain, or stages.

Constricted, *narrow* (_Ai_ 狹): a confined space or niche; one of six field positions; the limited extreme of the dimension distance; the opposite of **spread-out.**

Control, *govern* (_Chi_ 治): to manage situations; to overcome disorder; the opposite of **chaos.**

Dangerous: see **serious.**

Dangers, *adverse* (Ak 阨): a condition that makes it difficult to **advance**; one of three dimensions used to evaluate advantages; the dimension with the extreme field **positions** of **entangling** and **supporting**.

Death, *desperate* (*Si* 死): to end or the end of life or efforts; an extreme situation in which the only option is **battle**; one of nine **stages** or types of **terrain**; one of five types of **spies**; opposite of **survive**.

Deception, *bluffing, illusion* (*Gui* 詭): to control perceptions; to control information; to mislead an **enemy**; an attack on an opponent's **aim**; the characteristic of war that confuses perceptions.

Defend (*Shou* 守): to guard or to hold a **ground**; to remain in a **position**; the opposite of **attack**.

Detour (*Yu* 迂): the indirect or unsuspected path to a **position**; the more difficult path to **advantage**; the route that is not **direct**.

Direct, *straight* (*Jik* 直): a straight or obvious path to a goal; opposite of **detour**.

Distance, *distant* (*Yuan* 遠): the space separating **ground**; to be remote from the current location; to occupy **positions** that are not close to one another; one of six field positions; one of the three dimensions for evaluating opportunities; the emptiness of space.

Divide, *separate* (*Fen* 分): to break apart a larger force; to separate from a larger group; the opposite of **join** and **focus**.

Double agent, *reverse* (*Fan* 反): to turn around in direction; to change a situation; to switch a person's allegiance; one of five types of spies.

Easy, *light* (*Qing* 輕): to require little effort; a **situation** that requires little effort; one of nine **stages** or types of terrain; opposite of **serious**.

Emotion, *feeling* (*Xin* 心): an unthinking reaction to **aim**, a necessary element to inspire **moves**; a component of esprit de corps; never a sufficient cause for **attack**.

Enemy, *competitor* (*Dik* 敵): one who makes the same **claim**; one with a similar **goal**; one with whom comparisons of capabilities are made.

Entangling, *hanging* (*Gua* 縣): a **position** that cannot be returned to; any **condition** that leaves no easy place to go; one of six field positions.

Evade, *avoid* (*Bi* 避): the tactic used by small competitors when facing large opponents.

Fall apart, *collapse* (*Beng* 崩): to fail to execute good decisions; to fail to use a **constricted position**; one of six weaknesses of an organization.

Fall down, *sink* (*Haam* 陷): to fail to make good decisions; to **move** from a **supporting position**; one of six weaknesses of organizations.

Feelings, *affection, love* (*Ching* 情): the bonds of relationship; the result of a shared **philosophy**; requires management.

Fight, *struggle* (Dou 鬥): to engage in **conflict**; to face difficulties.

Fire (*Huo* 火): an environmental weapon; a universal analogy for all weapons.

Flee, *retreat, northward* (*Bei* 北): to abandon a **position**; to surrender **ground**; one of six weaknesses of an **army**; opposite of **advance**.

Focus, *concentrate* (*Zhuan* 專): to bring resources together at a given time; to **unite** forces for a purpose; an attribute of having a shared **philosophy**; the opposite of *divide*.

Force (*Lei* 力): power in the simplest sense; a **group** of people bound by **unity** and **focus**; the relative balance of **strength** in opposition to **weakness**.

Foresee: see **aim**.

Fullness: see **strength**.

General: see **leader**.

Goal: see **philosophy**.

Ground, *situation, stage* (*Di* 地): the earth; a specific place; a specific condition; the place one competes; the prize of competition; one of five key factors in competitive analysis; the opposite of **climate**.

Groups, *troops* (*Dui* 隊): a number of people united under a shared **philosophy**; human resources of an organization; one of the five targets of fire attacks.

Inside, *internal* (*Nei* 內): within a **territory** or organization; an insider; one of five types of spies; opposite of *Wai*, outside.

Intersecting, *highway* (*Qu* 衢): a **situation** or **ground** that allows you to **join**; one of nine types of terrain.

Join (*Hap* 合): to unite; to make allies; to create a larger **force**; opposite of **divide**.

Knowledge, *listening* (*Zhi*: 知): to have information; the result of listening; the first step in advancing a **position**; the basis of strategy.

Lax, *loosen* (*Shii* 弛): too easygoing; lacking discipline; one of six weaknesses of an army.

Leader, *general, commander* (*Jiang* 將): the decision-maker in a competitive unit; one who **listens** and **aims**; one who manages **troops**; superior of officers and men; one of the five key factors in analysis; the conceptual opposite of *fa*, the established methods, which do not require decisions.

Learn, *compare* (*Xiao* 效): to evaluate the relative qualities of **enemies**.

Listen, *obey* (*Ting* 聽): to gather **knowledge**; part of **analysis**.

Listening: see **knowledge**.

Local, *countryside* (_Xiang_ 鄉): the nearby **ground**; to have **knowledge** of a specific **ground**; one of five types of **spies**.

Marsh (_Ze_ 澤): **ground** where footing is unstable; one of the four types of **ground**; analogy for uncertain situations.

Method: see **system**.

Mission: see **philosophy**.

Momentum, *influence* (_Shi_ 勢): the **force** created by **surprise** set up by **standards;** used with **timing**.

Mountains, *hill, peak* (_Shan_ 山): uneven **ground**; one of four types of **ground**; an analogy for all unequal **situations**.

Move, *march, act* (_Hang_ 行): action toward a position or goal; used as a near synonym for _dong_, act.

Nation (_Guo_ 國): the state; the productive part of an organization; the seat of political power; the entity that controls an **army** or competitive part of the organization.

Obstacles, *barricaded* (_Xian_ 險): to have barriers; one of the three characteristics of the **ground**; one of six field positions; as a field position, opposite of **unobstructed**.

Open, *meeting, crossing* (_Jiao_ 來): to share the same **ground** without conflict; to come together; a **situation** that encourages a race; one of nine **terrains** or **stages**.

Opportunity: see _advantage._

Outmaneuver (_Sou_ 走): to go astray; to be **forced** into a **weak position**; one of six weaknesses of an army.

Outside, *external* (_Wai_ 外): not within a **territory** or **army**; one who has a different perspective; one who offers an objective view; opposite of **internal**.

Philosophy, *mission, goals* (_Tao_ 道): the shared **goals** that **unite** an **army**; a system of thought; a shared viewpoint; literally "the way"; a way to work together; one of the five key factors in **analysis**.

Plateau (_Liu_ 陸): a type of **ground** without defects; an analogy for any equal, solid, and certain **situation**; the best place for competition; one of the four types of **ground**.

Resources, *provisions* (_Liang_ 糧): necessary supplies, most commonly food; one of the five targets of fire attacks.

Restraint: see **timing.**

Reward, *treasure, money* (_Bao_ 賞): profit; wealth; the necessary compensation for competition; a necessary ingredient for **victory**; **victory** must pay.

Scatter, *dissipating* (_San_ 散): to disperse; to lose **unity**; the pursuit of separate **goals** as opposed to a central **mission**; a situation that causes a **force** to scatter; one of nine conditions or types of terrain.

Serious, *heavy* (_Chong_ 重): any task requiring effort and skill; a **situation** where resources are running low when you are deeply committed to a campaign or heavily invested in a project; a situation where opposition within an organization mounts; one of nine **stages** or types of **terrain.**

Siege (_Gong Cheng_ 攻城): to move against entrenched positions; any movement against an **enemy's strength**; literally "strike city"; one of the four forms of attack; the least desirable form of attack.

Situation: see **ground.**

Speed, *hurry* (Sai 馳): to **move** over **ground** quickly; the ability to **advance positions** in a minimum of time; needed to take advantage of a window of opportunity.

Spread-out, *wide* (_Guang_ 廣): a surplus of **distance**; one of the six **ground positions**; opposite of **constricted.**

Spy, *conduit, go-between* (_Gaan_ 間): a source of information; a channel of communication; literally, an "opening between."

Stage: see **ground.**

Standard, *proper, correct* (_Jang_ 正): the expected behavior; the standard approach; proven methods; the opposite of surprise; together with **surprise** creates **momentum.**

Storehouse, *house* (_Ku_ 庫): a place where resources are stockpiled; one of the five targets for fire attacks.

Stores, *accumulate, savings* (_Ji_ 糧): resources that have been stored; any type of inventory; one of the five targets of fire attacks.

Strength, *fullness, satisfaction* (_Sat_ 壹): wealth or abundance or resources; the state of being crowded; the opposite of Xu, empty.

Supply wagons, *transport* (_Zi_ 輜): the movement of **resources** through **distance**; one of the five targets of fire attacks.

Support, *supporting* (_Zhii_ 支): to prop up; to enhance; a **ground position** that you cannot leave without losing **strength**; one of six field positions; the opposite extreme of gua, entangling.

Surprise, *unusual, strange* (_Qi_ 奇) : the unexpected; the innovative; the opposite of **standard**; together with **standards** creates **momentum**.

Surround: see **confined**.

Survive, *live, birth* (_Shaang_ 生): the state of being created, started, or beginning; the state of living or surviving; a temporary condition of fullness; one of five types of spies; the opposite of **death**.

System, *method* (_Fa_ 法): a set of procedures; a group of techniques; steps to accomplish a **goal**; one of the five key factors in analysis; the realm of groups who must follow procedures; the opposite of the **leader**.

Territory, *terrain*: see **ground**.

Timing, *restraint* (_Jie_ 節): to withhold action until the proper time; to release tension; a companion concept to **momentum**.

Troops: see **group**.

Unity, *whole, oneness* (_Yi_ 一): the characteristic of a **group** that shares a **philosophy**; the lowest number; a **group** that acts as a unit; the opposite of **divided**.

Unobstructed, *expert* (_Tong_ 通): without obstacles or barriers; **ground** that allows easy movement; open to new ideas; one of six field positions; opposite of **obstructed**.

Victory, *win, winning* (_Sing_ 勝): success in an endeavor; getting a reward; serving your mission; an event that produces more than it consumes; to make a profit.

War, *competition, army* (Bing 兵): a dynamic situation in which **positions** can be won or lost; a contest in which a **reward** can be won; the conditions under which the principles of strategy work.

Water, *river* (_Shui_ 水): a fast-changing **ground**; fluid **conditions**; one of four types of **ground**; an analogy for change.

Weakness, *emptiness, need* (_Xu_ 虛): the absence of people or resources; devoid of **force**; the point of **attack** for an **advantage;** a characteristic of **ground** that enables **speed**; poor; the opposite of strength.

Win, *winning*: see **victory**.

Wind, *fashion, custom* (_Feng_ 風): the pressure of environmental forces.

The *Art of War Playbook* Series

There are over two-hundred and thirty articles on Sun Tzu's competitive principles in the nine volumes of the *Art of War Playbook*. Each volume covers a specific area of Sun Tzu strategy.

VOLUME ONE: - POSITIONS

VOLUME TWO: -PERSPECTIVE

VOLUME THREE: - OPPORTUNITIES

VOLUME FOUR: - PROBABILITY

VOLUME FIVE: - MISTAKES

VOLUME SIX: - SITUATIONS

VOLUME SEVEN: - MOMENTUM

VOLUME EIGHT: - REWARDS

VOLUME NINE: - VULNERABILITIES.

About the Translator and Author

Gary Gagliardi is recognized as America's leading expert on Sun Tzu's *The Art of War*. An award-winning author and business strategist, his many books on Sun Tzu's strategy have been translated around the world. He has appeared on hundreds of talk shows nationwide, providing strategic insight on the breaking news. He has trained decision makers from some of the world's most successful organizations in competitive thinking. His workshops convert Sun Tzu's many principles into a series of practical tools for handling common competitive challenges.

Gary began using Sun Tzu's competitive principles in a successful corporate career and when he started his own software company. In 1990, he wrote his first *Art of War* adaptation for his company's salespeople. By 1992, his company was on *Inc. Magazine's* list of the 500 fastest-growing privately held companies in America. He personally won the U.S. Chamber of Commerce Blue Chip Quality Award and was an Ernst and Young Entrepreneur of the Year finalist. His customers—AT&T, GE, and Motorola, among others—began inviting him to speak at their conferences. After becoming a multimillionaire when he sold his software company in 1997, he continued teaching *The Art of War* around the world.

Gary has authored several breakthrough works on *The Art of War*. Ten of his books on strategy have won book award recognition in nine different non-fiction categories.

Other *Art of War* Books
by Gary Gagliardi

Gary Gagliardi's Books are Available at:

SunTzus.com
Amazon.com
BarnesAndNoble.com
Itunes.apple.com

www.ingramcontent.com/pod-product-compliance
Lightning Source LLC
Chambersburg PA
CBHW070530200326
41519CB00013B/3003